Competing Through Talent

An Anthology

FOR THE TALENT-FOCUSED ENTERPRISE

BrassRing®
FOLLOW OUR LEAD.

Reprint permission list in Appendix.

First printed September 2002.

The paper used in this book meets the minimum requirements of the American National Standard for Information Services—Permanence of Paper for Printed Library Materials, ANSI Z39.48-1984

Library of Congress Control Number: 2002111007

Printed and bound in the United States of America.

BrassRing • 170 High StreetWaltham, MA • 02453

Contents

Chapter Two: Building Talent Relationships

Recruiting rules and techniques for building talent pool relationships, "net" speed competencies, and talent network efficiencies

Chapter Three: Nurturing Talent to Succeed and Stay

"Pre-hire to retire" best practice foundations and "how to" steps in maximizing an organization's people

Chapter Four: **Employer-of-Choice Organizations**

How organizations become employer-of-choice, keep pathways of communication open, revise traditional notions of "compensation," and emphasize talent career paths

Chapter Five: **Managing TRM Automation for Workplace Effectiveness**

Driving productivity by focusing not only on what technology can *do for the enterprise but what* can be done with *technology by the enterprise for greater ROI*

Acknowledgments

In addition to the thirty authors whose prolific words in this anthology serve to educate, motivate, and lead, BrassRing's visionary advisory board deserves special mention for its contributions to this project.

Special thanks go to book designer Bill Stanton whose award-winning book jackets and designs are always worthy of applause, and to Stephen Thomas whose enthusiasm and publishing acumen drives excellence across industries.

Project Lead and Acquisitions	CoChel Communication Strategies
Book/Jacket Design and Typesetting	Stanton Design
Production Coordination	Bookblock.org
Editorial Coordination	Windy Johnson
Publication Team	David Brennan
	Anne Culiner
	Sha Jones
	Eileen Lam
	Mark Lange
	Austin Whitman
Printer/Binder	Edwards Brothers, Inc.

Introduction

Talent is the mortar that holds your corporate mission and ideas together, brings product to market, and drives revenue and profitability. To understand Talent Relationship Management is to grasp the last, best opportunity to create and sustain competitive advantage.

It isn't getting easier. You've lived through—and need to find ways to prosper through—years of corporate restructuring, downsizing, mergers, and acquisitions . . . technological advances, market dislocation, accelerating customer expectations, and cycle times . . . and a fundamental change in the implied employment contract between employers and their people.

Today's workforce is more valuable because of what it knows. Companies that compete to win understand that labor is no longer just a commodity. Many are refocusing and reinventing their companies, attempting to run a lean enterprise and renew public trust in management. Most seek to attract, hire, contract, and develop people who possess specific knowledge, skill, and experience levels—and more important, are capable of a level of engagement with the company's goals that drives better financial results.

The anthology of articles before you underscores BrassRing's commitment to helping organizations understand and embrace the unique business imperatives emerging from a determination to compete not just "for" talent, but through talent.

Varied in scope and focus, each article offers specific strategies and actionable tactics. From Jenny Chatman's high-level view of the talent-focused enterprise culture, to Jac Fitz-enz's cutting-edge discussion on TRM leadership, I hope the book in your hands motivates both thought and action.

Individually and collectively, the authors in this anthology address best practice Talent Relationship Management priorities, processes, and technologies that add measurable value and competitive advantage to the enterprise.

I invite you to read on.

Deborah M. Besemer
Chief Executive Officer
BrassRing

CHAPTER ONE

Talent as a Strategic Imperative

> "The great thing in this world is not so much where we are, but in what direction we are moving."

—Oliver Wendell Holmes

1

Executing Organizational Strategy Through a Talent-Focused Culture[1]

JENNIFER A. CHATMAN PhD

Jennifer A. Chatman PhD is the Harold Furst Professor in Management Philosophy and Values at the Haas School of Business at UC Berkeley. During the 2001-02 academic year, she was the Marvin Bower Fellow at the Harvard Business School. From 1987 to 1993 Dr. Chatman was on the faculty of the Kellogg Graduate School of Management, Northwestern University. Her research and consulting work continue to focus on the business advantages of leveraging organizational culture and leading change and have been highlighted in *Business Week*, *Fortune*, *Inc.*, *The Jungle*, the *San Francisco Chronicle*, the *Los Angeles Times*, and *Working Mother*. She is a member of the Academy of Management, the American Psychological Association, the American Psychological Society, and the Society for Industrial and Organizational Behavior. Dr. Chatman can be reached at chatman@haas.berkeley.edu.

A *Fortune* magazine article highlighting path-breaking research by Ram Charan and Geoffrey Colvin (1999) led with a provocative cover—"Why CEOs Fail". The definitive answer had been found, and it was notoriously simple: CEOs failed when they failed to execute their strategy. This was an amazing conclusion because, in contrast to what industrial economists have been telling us for years—that firms with well-formulated and hard-to-imitate business strategies emerge as the winners (e.g., Porter, 1980)—Charan and Colvin's article suggested that firms with merely reasonable strategies who execute fully on those could be the most successful.

This shifts our focus from strategy formulation to strategy *execution*, and organizational culture is all about execution. Consider the often-cited example of Southwest Airlines, a company with a transparent, almost simple, strategy: high volume; short, convenient flights; using only fuel efficient 737s; culminating in low costs and the ability to offer customers low-priced tickets. And yet, Southwest has been the only US airline to be profitable for twenty-eight consecutive years (Laing, 2001). One key to Southwest's success is its remarkably short turnaround time, fifteen minutes versus competitors' average of thirty-five minutes (O'Reilly & Pfeffer, 1995). Planes don't sit long at the jet way. Instead, employees across functional lines band together to get the planes out quickly, despite being 89 percent unionized. This results in an average plane utilization of around twelve hours at Southwest versus the industry average of closer to nine hours. Southwest's success hinges not on how brilliant, unique, or opaque their strategy is, but on the alignment between their culture and strategy, and how clearly employees understand and care about that culture.

Unfortunately, the term organizational culture has become faddish, and, like all good fads, has been overused and under-defined. The goal here is to precisely clarify why culture is powerful and provide specific criteria for developing a strong, strategically relevant culture, one that is talent-focused and likely to enhance your organization's performance. Talent Relationship Management (TRM) provides a framework through which an effective culture is developed and maintained. These include (1) who firms hire, for example Southwest culls through 140,000 applications looking for those who best fit its culture to fill 5000 jobs; (2) how firms clarify what is important, for example the training and socialization process that help Southwest employees fully appreciate just how important keeping costs low and customers happy is; and (3) how firms reward and recognize people for culturally consistent performance. The bottom line is simple: by actively managing culture, your organization and the people working within it will be more likely to deliver on strategic objectives over the long haul.

Why Is Organizational Culture Powerful?

Focusing People Intensely on Strategy Execution

So what is culture? Simply put, culture is a system of shared values defining what is important, and norms, defining appropriate attitudes and behaviors, that guide members' attitudes and behaviors (O'Reilly & Chatman, 1996: 166). Culture is more specific than vision in that a good vision engages employees emotionally by setting up motivating overarching goals to which they can aspire. For example, Citigroup's admirable vision, "We want to be seen as one of the most respected financial institutions in the world, as a unique global full-service bank," can be seen throughout the organization. The bank is global—located in ninety-four different countries for nearly 100 years, and full-service as evidenced by its recent merger with Travelers. But, if you work for Citigroup and wake up one morning saying, "Ok, today's the day—I'm going to be really global," it's not clear exactly what this would mean. Culture operates at the level of daily beliefs and behavior to translate abstract visions into useful information about how to behave and what decisions and tradeoffs to make.

An effective culture is also closely related to business strategy. Strategy focuses on the specific business objectives such as your target market, the products or services you offer, and how you compete. Indeed, you cannot craft an organizational culture until you fully develop and articulate your business strategy; strategy must come first. Thus, our first criterion for using culture as a leadership tool is that it must be *strategically relevant*.

Formal Versus Social Control: The Power of Shared Cultural Norms

Norms, or legitimate, socially shared standards against which the appropriateness of behavior can be evaluated (Birenbaum & Sagarin, 1976), are the psychological bases of culture. Norms are distinct from rules, which are formal, codified directives. The concept of norms also implies social control; that is, norms act as positive or negative means of ensuring conformity and applying sanctions to deviant behavior (e.g., O'Reilly & Chatman, 1996).

One study, conducted some years ago, unequivocally demonstrates the power of social norms. Some epidemiologists were interested in hand-washing behavior in public restrooms and so they set up a controlled experiment in which unsuspecting members of the public who entered public restrooms either found another person in the restroom (actually a confederate of the experiment—condition 1), or no one else (condition 2). In condition 2 the researchers had rigged up a video camera to record hand-washing behavior. Their research question was, of course, will there be a difference in the incidence of hand-washing across these two conditions? The results were amazing; about 90 percent of people who were in the restroom with the confederate washed up; when people were alone, however, only 15 percent washed their hands! The message is simple: We are so influenced by other's expectations, specifically their expectations that we uphold shared social norms (in this case, the norm of hygiene), that we are willing and likely to alter our behavior in their presence, that is, to do something different than we would do if we were alone. We assimilate because the consequences of violating strong norms—at best embarrassment, and, at worst, exclusion or alienation from the social group—threaten our ability to survive in an interdependent world.

How then, do norms work in today's organizations? Consider an example from Nordstrom, a strong culture organization known for its emphasis on customer service. Recently Lance, a polite and attentive sales associate, showed me nine pairs of shoes. Unfortunately, the store did not have the size/color/style combination that I wanted. As I was leaving, another sales associate, Howard, approached and suggested that he call a few other Nordstrom stores to find the shoes. Ten minutes later, Howard excitedly informed me that, though he had not found the shoes at another Nordstrom store, he did find them at a nearby Macy's (a primary Nordstrom competitor). Rather than sending me to Macy's, Howard had already arranged for the shoes to be overnight mailed to my home. "Of course," Howard informed me, "Macy's will bill you for the shoes, but Nordstrom will pay for the overnight delivery charge." Howard understood the importance of customer service and was willing to go above and beyond the call of duty to ensure that even Lance's customer was completely satisfied. But, the most interesting part of the story occurred next. While leaving Nordstrom, I eavesdropped on a conversation that I was clearly not supposed to hear. Howard had gone back to Lance and said, "I can't believe you didn't work harder to find those shoes for her. You really let *us* down." Remember, Howard is not Lance's boss—they are peers—and yet, the norms encouraging customer service at Nordstrom are so strong that members are willing to sanction each other, regardless of level, for a failure to uphold those norms.

Nordstrom prides itself on providing, not average or good, but *outstanding* customer service. The problem is that relying on formal rules, policies, and procedures will not result in outstanding anything, be it customer service, innovation, or quality. Think back to the last time you had a peak consumer experience—you were "wowed" by someone or an organization—what impressed you? When I ask people this question they typically talk about how someone went above and beyond the call of duty to solve *their specific problem*. Formal rules are useful for standardizing performance and avoiding having to relearn things each time. But they are only useful for addressing situations that are *predictable and regular*. In contrast, outstanding service is determined, in customer's eyes, by how you deal with situations that are nearly impossible to anticipate, unique to a particular person, and difficult to solve.

The irony of leading through culture is that the less formal direction you give employees about how to execute strategy, the more ownership they take over their actions and the better they perform. New employees at Nordstrom are told simply to, "Use your good judgment in all situations." (Spector & McCarthy, 1995: 16), and at Southwest to, "Do what it takes to make the Customer happy" (O'Reilly & Pfeffer, 1995: 7). Employees have to be freed up from rules in order to deliver fully on strategic objectives; they have to understand the ultimate strategic goals and the norms through which they can be successfully achieved, and they must *care* about reaching those goals and what their coworkers will think of them if they don't. Strong norms increase members' clarity about priorities and expectations, and their bonds with one another. Unlike formal rules, policies and procedures, culture empowers employees to think and act on their own in pursuit of strategic objectives, increasing their commitment to those goals. Violations are considered in terms of letting their colleagues down rather than breaking rules. The payoff is huge: If Howard is monitoring his own behavior against Nordstrom's strategic objectives—*and Lance's*—their manager does not have to spend time looking over their shoulders and can, instead, focus on the really important work of leadership: planning for the next strategic challenge and supporting employees so they can do an outstanding job. Thus, the second criterion for using culture as a leadership tool is that it be *strong*.

What Makes Culture Strong?

Strong cultures are based on two characteristics, high levels of agreement among employees about what's valued, and high levels of intensity; that is, people care about upholding these values. If both are high, a strong culture exists, and if both are low, the culture is not strong at all. Some organizations are characterized by high levels of intensity but low levels of agreement, or what could be called "warring factions" (O'Reilly, 1989). Within many high-tech firms such intensity exists but groups disagree about priorities. For example, marketing groups typically focus on customer driven product features while engineering groups focus on elegant product designs. More common, however, are organizations in which members agree about what's important, but they don't much care, and as such, are unwilling to go the extra mile (e.g., take a risk, stay late) to deliver on strategic objectives or to sanction others for a failure to uphold those norms. These are called "vacuous" cultures (O'Reilly, 1989) and their frequency probably reflects the faddish nature of organizational culture and the lip service such organizations pay to it. Most organizations are aware of the importance of managing culture, but in their attempt to jump on the culture bandwagon, are unable to develop the clarity, consistency, and comprehensiveness that encourage employees to care intensely about executing strategic objectives.

Building and Managing a Talent-Focused Organizational Culture

The contribution to bottom line performance of strategically relevant, strong cultures has been supported by substantial empirical and applied evidence (e.g., Kotter & Heskett, 1992). The key question, however, is how can your organization develop, manage, and change your culture to meet these criteria and promote extraordinary performance? The answer lies, quite simply, in how you manage your talent. TRM systems and strategies enable you to combine the *art* of finding the best candidate "fit" with the science of data analysis, process automation, and decision support; helping you to maximize your only truly indispensable competitive asset: people. There are at least three levers for managing a talent-focused culture—whom you select, how you socialize, orient and train recruits, and how you reward and recognize employees. Each is described briefly below.[2]

Tool #1: Recruiting and Selecting People for Culture Fit

Selection is the process of choosing new members (for organizations) and choosing to join a particular organization (for job candidates). My approach to selection contrasts with typical approaches by emphasizing person-culture fit in addition to person-job fit (Chatman, 1991). This requires anticipating whether the culture your firm emphasizes will be inherently rewarding for potential recruits.

Consider, for example, General Electric's description of desirable candidates, who "stimulate and relish change and are not frightened or paralyzed by it, seeing change as an opportunity, not a threat," and "have a passion for excellence, hating bureaucracy, and all the nonsense that comes with it." Note the intensity of the language, which does not focus on which computer programs people know or their geographic preferences, but rather, their thirst for challenge and change. These are qualities that differentiate between people who are, and are not, successful at GE. Firms

There are at least three levers for managing a talent-focused culture—whom you select, how you socialize, orient and train recruits, and how you reward and recognize employees.

often get caught focusing exclusively on hiring people whose skills fit their entry-level jobs, and yet, if a person is successful, he or she will hold multiple jobs within the firm. These jobs are linked, not by some universal set of skills, but rather, by the organizational culture. Therefore, it makes sense to hire people who will fit the culture, possibly even trading off some immediate skills necessary for the specific entry job for better culture fit. People can learn new skills; establishing cultural fit is much harder.

Second, be mindful of recruiter characteristics (Connerley & Rynes, 1997). A fundamental theory in psychology is the "similarity-attraction effect" (e.g., Berscheid & Reis, 1998). We are attracted to people who are similar to ourselves. Why? Well, most of us like ourselves, think we're doing a pretty good job, and wouldn't mind having lunch with ourselves now and then. So, when you ask us to recruit new members, we are likely to pick people just like us! The message is simple but important: Be careful which people you send out to do your recruiting because they will bring more of "them" back!

Third, consider your selection process in light of your culture. How, for example, did Cisco Systems ensure high culture fit despite facing Silicon Valley's brutally competitive labor market in the late 1990s, hiring an average of 1000 new employees through small acquisitions and individual recruiting *every month*? First, they developed culturally consistent selection criteria targeting candidates who were frugal, enthusiastic about the future of the Internet, smart, and not consumed with status (O'Reilly, 1998). Second, they conducted benchmarking studies and focus groups, so that the selection process was maximally effective in getting the people they wanted (Beck, 2000). Third, they targeted "passive applicants," people who are satisfied in their current jobs and not job hunting but who might be lured to Cisco, and developed a convenient website for them to learn about Cisco. Noticing that they were getting over 500,000 hits per month during work hours, Cisco made sure that the website was fast and easy to use; for example, the initial application took five minutes to complete.

---

*At E*Trade, which was founded in 1996 and grew to become the number two on-line brokerage by 1999, new employees are asked to stand up on a chair at their first staff meeting and tell everyone something embarrassing about themselves.*

Applicants who pressed a "friends@Cisco" hot key got a call from a current Cisco employee at a comparable level within 24 hours (O'Reilly, 1998). These discussions typically focused on the hard-to-convey culturally relevant information that, because of the similarity of the source to the candidate, provided credible information about what it is really like to work at Cisco. Cisco aggressively pursued and won desired candidates by constructing a comprehensive, culturally relevant selection process.

Tool #2: Managing Culture Through Intensive Socialization and Training

Socialization is the process by which an individual comes to understand the values, abilities, expected behaviors, and social knowledge that are essential for assuming an organization role and participating as an organization member. Socialization and selection processes are somewhat substitutable (Chatman, 1991). In tight labor markets, firms need to rely more on socializing people once they join, and, conversely, when labor is more freely available and firms can be highly selective, they will not need to invest as much in socialization practices. Much is known about effective socialization practices (e.g., Pfeffer, 1998). Two key aspects of socialization are particularly important; ensuring that employees acquire cultural knowledge and that they bond with one another.

At E*Trade, which was founded in 1996 and grew to become the number two on-line brokerage by 1999, new employees are asked to stand up on a chair at their first staff meeting and tell everyone something embarrassing about themselves (Lee, 2000). Though a slightly bizarre practice, it jibes with sound psychological logic. Once newcomers disclose this embarrassing thing about themselves, asking questions about their new job or company won't be nearly as embarrassing. Newcomers will be much more likely to ask their new colleagues for the information they need to hit the ground running in their new job without worrying about a loss of face since they already lost their face at that first meeting! Newcomers are grateful that their new colleagues accept them despite their faults. Further, knowing that others have gone through this unique initiation rite creates a bond that allows members to work together more effectively, and, by increasing their accountability to others, makes it more likely that newcomers will work hard to uphold established organizational norms. E*Trade's CEO, Christos Cotsakos, has also taken his executive team Formula One racing to make them "move faster," and enrolled them in cooking school to increase their agility in working together (Lee, 2000). These practices promote the two goals of socialization: clarifying the cultural values and creating strong bonds among employees so that they are accountable to one another for upholding those values.

Tool #3: Managing Culture Through the Reward System

Culture is an organization's informal reward system, and needs to be intricately connected to formal rewards. At CompUSA, the largest retailer and reseller of personal computer related products and services in the United States; CEO James Halpin has created "a cross between a college fraternity and a military boot camp" (Puffer, 1999: 29). The company's strategic focus on revenue is extremely salient, sometimes encompassed in rather uncomfortable practices. For example, regional sales managers attending quarterly meetings are assigned a seat at the U-shaped table according to their store sales, with those with the lowest sales being assigned to the tables nearest the front because, as Halpin says, "they have to listen to everything we've got to say" (Puffer, 1999: 33). Name badges include a person's name and their stores' "shrink number," or inventory losses due to theft or accounting errors. On the positive reinforcement side, when employees make large commissions—such as when a young employee made $50,000 in commission in one month—Halpin travels to their store to deliver the cash to them personally, in front of customers and other employees. Though these specific rewards (and punishments) may be inappropriate for your organization, the lesson is that rewards need to be clear, consistent, and comprehensive—the focus on revenues at CompUSA is simply impossible for employees to miss.

Developing a Talent-Focused Culture: Some Conclusions

Using culture as a business tool requires that it is *talent focused*, by being relevant to your strategic objectives and strong.

TRM can help you develop and manage a talent-focused culture. You should use TRM systems and strategies to help make decisions about whom you recruit and select, how you reinforce your organization's culture as well as current employees, and as you develop a market for internal succession.

Managing culture requires using a TRM-centric selection approach; the selection experience is the first opportunity for recruits to learn about what is important in your organization.

Culture "works" when it is consistent and comprehensive, across the entire employee lifecycle.

Organizational culture can be a powerful force that clarifies what's important and coordinates members' efforts without the costs and inefficiencies of close supervision. Culture also identifies an organization's distinctive competence to external constituencies. Managing culture requires using a TRM-centric selection approach; the selection experience is the first opportunity for recruits to learn about what is important in your organization. Training, socialization, and rewards should be used as opportunities to continually convey important values to organizational members.

One thing is guaranteed: A culture will form in your organization, your group, and your department. In fact, it already has. The question is whether it is one that helps or hinders your ability to execute your strategic objectives. Organizational culture is too important to leave to chance—use your TRM-focused culture to fully execute your strategy and inspire innovation at your company.

References

Beck, B. (2000, March). *Cisco Systems*. Class presentation, Haas School of Business, Berkeley, CA.

Berscheid, E., & Reis, H.T. (1998). Attraction and close relationships. In D.T. Gilbert, S.T. Fiske, & G. Lindzey (Eds.), *The Handbook of Social Psychology* (4th ed., pp. 193-281). New York: McGraw-Hill.

Birenbaum, A., & Sagarin, E. (1976). *Norms and Human Behavior*. New York: Praeger.

Charan, R., & Colvin, G. (1999, June 21). *Why CEOs Fail*. Fortune, 139, 68-78.

Chatman, J. A. (1991). Matching people and organizations: Selection and socialization in public accounting firms. *Administrative Science Quarterly*, 36, 459-484.

Chatman, J. & Cha, S. (forthcoming, 2003). Leading through leveraging culture. To appear in, S. Chowdhury (Ed.), *Next Generation Business Series: Leadership*, Financial Times-Prentice Hall Publishers.

Connerley, M. L. & Rynes, S. L. (1997). The influence of recruiter characteristics and organizational recruitment support on perceived recruiter effectiveness: Views from applicants and recruiters. *Human Relations*, 50, 1563-1586.

Kotter, J. P., & Heskett, J. L. (1992). *Corporate Culture and Performance*. New York: Free Press.

Laing, J. R. (2001, July 2). Nothing but blue skies. *Barron's, 81*, 25-29.

Lee, L. (2000, February 7). Tricks of E*Trade: In his drive to create a Net powerhouse, Christos Cotsakos is building a culture that's edgy, a bit bizarre-and often brilliant. *Business Week*, p. EB18.

O'Reilly, C. (1989). Corporations, culture, and commitment: Motivation and social control in organizations. *California Management Review*, 31, 9-25.

O'Reilly, C. (1998). Cisco Systems: The acquisition of technology is the acquisition of people. Case # HR-10, Graduate School of Business, Stanford University.

O'Reilly, C., & Chatman, J. (1996). Cultures as social control: Corporations, cults, and commitment. In L. Cummings, & B. Staw (Eds.), *Research in Organizational Behavior* (Vol. 18, pp. 157-200). Greenwich, CT: JAI Press.

O'Reilly, C., & Pfeffer, J. (1995). Southwest Airlines: Using human resources for competitive advantage (A). HR-1A. Graduate School of Business, Stanford University.

Pfeffer, J. (1981). *Power In Organizations*. Marshfield, MA, Pitman Pub.

Pfeffer, J. (1998). *The Human Equation: Building Profits by Putting People First*. Boston: Harvard Business School Press.

Porter, M. E. (1980). *Competitive Strategy: Techniques for Analyzing Industries and Competitors*. New York: Free Press.

Puffer, S. (1999). CompUSA's CEO James Halpin on technology, rewards, and commitment. *Academy of Management Executive*, 13, 29-36.

Spector, R., & McCarthy, P. D. (1995). *The Nordstrom Way*. New York: John Wiley & Sons.

Tushman, M. L., & O'Reilly, C. A. (1997). *Winning Through Innovation: A Practical Guide to Leading Organizational Change and Renewal*. Boston: Harvard Business School Press.

Footnotes

1. Portions of this paper were excerpted from Chatman, J. & Cha, S. (forthcoming, 2003). *Leading Through Leveraging Culture.* To appear in, S. Chowdhury (Ed.), *Next Generation Business Series: Leadership*, Financial Times-Prentice Hall Publishers.
2. For greater detail on these three tools, see, Chatman, 1991; Chatman & Cha, 2002; O'Reilly, 1989; O'Reilly & Chatman, 1996; and Tushman & O'Reilly, 1997.

> “What is obscure, we eventually see. What is obvious, usually takes a longer time.”

—Edward R. Murrow

1

Automating Employment Management: TRM, the New Generation

H. MICHAEL BOYD PhD

H. Michael Boyd PhD is an internationally recognized expert in the field of human resources with over thirty years of corporate and consulting experience. Dr. Boyd is Principal and Founder of Boyd Associates, a HR strategy consulting firm and is a Professor of Management and Organizational Behavior at Bentley College in Waltham, Massachusetts. He is the host of the "Human Resources Issues" discussion board on Monster and a content consultant to IDC. The current president of EMA, New England region, Dr. Boyd can be reached at boyd@boydassociates.net.

Introduction

In the "good old days"—back in the 1980s and 1990s—companies could rely on establishing a good brand and a good recruiting process to hire the talent that they needed to succeed. While they were not always successful, the strategy was one accepted as solid and competitive. The workforce and the workplace, however, have changed in the past several years and new technologies and tools are being applied to extend the reach of the employment function. One of the new concepts and tool sets is "talent relationship management." BrassRing, Inc. has built a set of tools around the concept that the relationship with talent must be more than about the initial hiring activity.

There were two converging applications of computing that began long before the talent wars of the 90s. One area of activity is what is now called "CRM (customer relationship management). It is not a new idea. Retailers and businesses have always captured and used individual customer preferences and information to delight and satisfy customer needs and desires. That was the very foundation of competition prior to mass-retailing. It was the local drug store, movie theater, or clothing store. Merchants would know their customers and stock what their customers liked. When was the last time that Wal-Mart called to tell you that the red licorice that you like had come in? Customers have traded the personal touch for price and variety. Merchants can offer lower prices and stock enough variety that most customers will find what they need.

Of course, merchants and businesses, being competitive, began trying to reach out to stimulate sales by using categorized lists based on what you had bought or self-disclosed. The practices became overwhelming and began alienating rather than satisfying customers. CRM is an automated effort at collecting data about customers and deriving from it a much more accurate listing of what a customer would want to be told about. It does seem to be working well for many enterprises—profit, non-profit, government, academic, and others.

The concept of CRM is beginning to be applied to the labor market much as it has been to the product and services marketing world. As the labor markets and individual workers have taken on an increased importance and value over the past decade so too has the desire to be able to attract individuals that have specific experience, characteristics, skills, knowledge, and interests. The new holistic approach to recruiting / staffing / employment has been dubbed TRM (talent relationship management) by employment automation and services leader BrassRing, Inc.

TRM

As with CRM, TRM is not a new concept and many best-in-class enterprises are very good at it. One kind of TRM that has been working well is the use of employee referrals for employment. Rather than using a computer to collect and assess information about potential employees it relies on the brains of other employees—so, I suppose that is a biotechnical form of TRM. Long-term, of course, it is not very efficient. The value of applying computing resources to the collection, maintenance, and assessment of worker information is the same as with customer or vendor information. It provides the ability to target potential candidates for specific work with great accuracy in a way that will meet all of that person's needs. With this information the employment professional may concentrate on the employee-employer relationship rather than the process of identifying potential candidates.

Companies that turn to BrassRing are often those that find significant added value in building a broader relationship with talent than they have with other disparate employment automation tools and service resources.

BrassRing, Inc. is a leading provider of employment management and automation systems and resources. They have a unique collection of resources that attend to the integration of employment activities which allow movement toward real talent relationship management. Their TRM oriented product and service offerings include: Enterprise and Talent Gateways; selected partners who provide complimentary on-line recruiting and staffing services; a Professional Services Group which addresses needs for expert staffing assessment, diagnosis, planning, and project resources; niche job boards; and leading career events and recruiting job fairs. Companies that turn to BrassRing are often those that find significant added value in building a broader relationship with talent than they have with other disparate employment automation tools and service resources.

Employment Automation

Employment automation has been around for a very long time. Like most functions it was initially, in the 60s and 70s, a way of keeping records, sending letters, and creating forms. In the 1980s applicant tracking systems were designed in order to collect, track, and report enterprise-wide staffing activity data. In the 1990s new web-centric tools allowed the interface to recruiting data to become available and useful to recruiters, HR managers, line managers, administrators, and even employees. Many can remember when the great innovation in employment administration was the introduction of NCR paper which replaced the need for carbon paper. So, we have progressed in about a thirty-year period from carbon paper to word processing to applicant tracking systems to "webified" enterprise employment solutions.

Complex Administrative Requirements

The administrative aspects of a good employment function are often overwhelming. As a result, they are often left undone. The results of poor administration are:

- Poor and incomplete records
- Inability to develop strategies
- Lack of effective tactical planning
- Poor recruiting practices
- Non-competitive recruiting results
- A recruiting function that commands little or no respect from line managers, employees, applicants, or other HR professionals.

There are legal and statutory requirements that certain data about applicants for employment be collected, recorded, maintained, and available upon request. There are also requirements that certain information about applicants for employment may not be collected and used. Collecting and maintaining information such as age (in the US) or race may put the company at considerable risk. It is critical that information be collected accurately, consistently, and in strict accordance with desired practice. Of course, nothing is simple and this area is no exception. It is necessary for the organization to report the racial, gender, etc. make up of its applicants but, at the same time, be able to substantiate that the information was not a factor in employment decision making (except where race, gender, age, etc. are legitimate and valid factors).

The larger the organization, the more important is administrative accuracy and effectiveness. Incorrect data, missing data, or late data will always cause the system to fail.

The value of information in TRM is exceptional. The more a recruiter or hiring manager knows about a candidate the more likely they are going to be able to select a potential top performing contributor. They must also create an individual value proposition for that top performer that will convince him or her to join the company. Neither the hiring decision nor the acceptance of the offer can be optimally accomplished without excellent information. Companies with good information consistently outperform companies without good information in the competition for talent. Companies with excellent employment administrative systems, practices, and discipline invariably have the best information. Even the best recruiter is at a severe competitive disadvantage without excellent information. The manager of an employment function simply can't manage without it—period!

Employment Systems

There are many employment automation systems and services. This abundance of suppliers has created a very competitive landscape for the employment automation and services provider industry. The key for an employment function is to select a way of creating administrative excellence that will be persistent, pervasive, and exact. Some companies will be best served by a large, integrated, legacy system. Many companies are better off having a small applicant tracking system on a PC on the employment administrator's desk. There are many more disasters than successes caused by making the wrong choice, or at least a choice that was not workable for that particular company. It is too easy to assume that all employment functions and activities are the same. They are not and the amount of difference between them is crucial to understand and accommodate when selecting and implementing any system.

The key is often the underlying employment processes that are being automated. While the technical aspects of a system are certainly important to its implementation and support, it is really the company's employment processes and the discipline of its administrative practices and requirements that enable a system to succeed or cause it to fail.

TRM Is a Paradigm and a Process, Not Simply a System

The focus of this paper is on the concept of TRM as the new paradigm in the area of employment and talent relationships. There are always dangers of letting automation take the place of human interaction and understanding. Those functions and companies will fail. Work is a social phenomenon. As such, the real engagement mechanism is interpersonal involvement. Where automation prevents that in the employment process it will cause the process to break down and fail. TRM emphasizes the extended and individual relationship that must be constructed for each and every employee.

The success of BrassRing, as an example, indicates that the employer and employment professional community agree that TRM is indeed the new generation of employment thinking and that it needs employment systems and services that focus on relationships in addition to the important traditional attention to applicant tracking functionality.

Of course, even the best tools will not save a self-destructive set of company priorities. A good illustration is the practice in America of firing (layoff, downsizing, reduction in force, and other more socially palatable terms) employees in order to reduce the operating cost of the enterprise when the company is not in danger of failure. The old approach is to fire them and provide some minimal financial and job hunting support (Although there have been many harsh practices of late where no severance and no notice were provided to fired employees.). I believe that those practices will prevent a company from participating in the labor markets of the future.

The companies that will be able to employ the workforce that they need at any time will be the ones that have adopted and live a TRM philosophy—they will have enduring relationships with candidates that were not hired, employees, former employees, retired employees, and employee affinity groups which will allow them welcome access to needed labor.

The smart company is the one that will not terminate employees when business revenues fall.

The smart company is the one that will not terminate employees when business revenues fall. They are companies like Agilent which cut salaries 10 percent across the board to avoid laying off employees. That is a wonderful example of TRM because TRM starts at the top and the Aligent action follows the example of one of its founders, Bill Hewlett, who once mandated that every employee take Fridays off (including himself) for six months to avoid laying off 1000 employees during a major sales downturn. There are other great examples of TRM such as MFS Investment management in Boston which hadn't laid people off in seventy years. The key is simply that these companies respect and value the human contributors in the business more than they do the capital metrics of the business. The business metrics, of course, are crucially important but the people are simply more valued. Those firms will prevail. Others will cease to exist and no one will care to come to the funeral.

Conclusion

As consumers are becoming more accustomed to individualized, desired, and non-invasive solicitations and targeting they will also begin expecting desired, individualized, and non-invasive contacting relative to their careers, work, and employment. This aspect of contact is much more sensitive due to regulations, personal privacy, appropriateness, and timing. In the US society issues of self worth and self esteem also come heavily into play with the subject of one's job or position; and on a global basis the core issues of security, predictability, and dignity are always part of the consideration. Work and employment relationships are complex, perhaps more complex than any other aspect of social experience.

It is therefore absolutely necessary that the outreach aspect of TRM be of the highest sensitivity. To accomplish that requires the kind of data, information, and process excellence that has been noted earlier in this paper. Without it TRM will be a dysfunctional and negative effort. Systems and resources that attend to that information excellence are absolutely necessary. Solutions that enable the building and maintenance of relationships with talent are critical for companies that desire to compete for a decreasing supply of skilled professionals over the next decade.

The companies with talent relationships will know who to call when they need help. The companies without those relationships just won't have anyone to call.

> "Many times a day I realize how much my own life is built upon the labors of my fellow men . . ."

—Albert Einstein

1

Talent Relationship Management
The Last Source of Competitive Advantage

MARK LANGE

Mark Lange, Vice President, marketing & business development for BrassRing Systems, has eighteen years of experience in workforce policy and technology business development. As chief speechwriter to two United States Secretaries of Labor (Ann McLaughlin and Elizabeth Dole), he defined and positioned US policy in the 1980s on workforce and competitiveness challenges—particularly the impact of the skills gap and technical employee shortages on corporate productivity. Since joining BrassRing Systems in 1997, the company has grown to a position of market leadership as the largest provider of Talent Relationship Management systems. Mr. Lange holds an MBA from Stanford University and a BA from Dartmouth. Mr. Lange can be reached at mlange@brassring.com.

Most managers intuitively grasp the importance of people. Any company's website will suggest that their people are their most important asset. And as part of sweeping investments in information technology, many firms have implemented point solutions for erecruiting, administration, performance assessment, employee self-service, and the like—generally fragmented, but at least taking the important first step of eliminating paper-based processes and speeding workflow.

Very few organizations, however, understand how to implement process technology that creates meaningful connections and feedback loops between the people it recruits and retains; their development, performance, and mobility within the firm; and the firm's operating and financial results.

You'll soon be hearing more about companies that do—and you'll see it reflected in their stock price. For the rest of this decade, a defining characteristic of competitive success will be how an organization identifies, recruits, engages, develops, retains, and re-deploys talent—in all of its forms, and at every stage of the business cycle and the talent life cycle.

Within the broad domain of human capital management—at the intersection between people, technology, data, and process management—a new discipline is emerging. Talent Relationship Management (TRM) is a practice being honed and refined by IT and HR leaders that are linking formerly disconnected domains, enabling collaborative workflow through the intelligent application of technology, and driving enterprise wide visibility into the ultimate source of an organization's success.

The goals of this article are to challenge the way you think about talent, technology, and competition, provide a few ways to bring those words on the website to life, and highlight process technology that will make sure those well-intentioned managers are following more than their instincts.

Why Talent is Strategic

In most minds, the "value" of talent tends to be framed in terms of direct costs and opportunity costs—the lost productivity of open positions. And on the basis of direct cost alone, the story is staggering.

Consider the current 12 percent average annual turnover of 23 million US salaried employees averaging US $30,000 per year[1]—with a direct recruiting and replacement cost conservatively estimated at three months' salary. Add the additional 90 million hourly employees turning over at an average of 68 percent a year at a direct cost of US $2,961 each.[2]

That totals US $253.7 billion a year for the US alone—close to 10 percent of GDP. Clearly, even marginal process improvements have profound economic consequences for American companies.

Executives understand costs. But the cost focus, particularly in recruiting, misses the larger point: talent is strategic. In fact, it is the singular factor that ensures every other form of capital investment—product, infrastructure, systems, technology, and hard assets—pays off. Behind the tremendous productivity improvements enabled by information technology are the people that do all of the knowing, building, planning, collaborating, executing, supporting, and competing.

How well should an organization deploy and manage the one asset that ensures that every other investment pays off? As well as it can—and most could do far better than they are. Making that case in the executive suite is a critical element in the ascending relevance of HR in world-class organizations. Doing so is a path to a more meaningful seat at the table, and a more substantial role in corporate governance.

Why Almost Nobody Does Enough About Talent

The high-level objective—identifying high performers and helping them be their most effective—is clear. So why doesn't HR drive this agenda aggressively? In part, keeping the administrative trains running on time consumes every available resource. The average HR department operates on 0.5 to 1 percent of revenue, and is under increasing pressure to do more with less. HR headcounts shrunk by as much as 50 percent over the course of the 1990s.[3]

But remember, it was only twenty years ago that the discipline of HR grew out of "personnel" and started focusing on measurement, deliverables, output, results—rather than simply inputs, programs, budgets, and costs. Tremendous progress has been made with technology to automate transactions and push tasks out to the line. Some firms have taken the typical HR ratio (one staff per 100 employees) and raised it to 1:150—while improving service delivery through automation.

The deeper reason that many in HR may not have been able to make talent a strategic priority in the executive suite is a tendency, at those elevations, to regard people as another "inventory" to be managed (and in a recession, blown out the door at a loss). The short-term unemployment rate tends to whipsaw perception and muddy thinking about talent. In a contraction, it's too easy to think: "The economy is cooling off; at least we won't have so much trouble recruiting." Stay tuned . . .

What Talent Shortage?

The current economic slow-down may take some of the heat off —in sectors more than others—but it's only an opportunity to change the wheels on the car at thirty-five miles per hour, before they spin back up to seventy-five again.

In the near-term, Forrester Research sees the overall slump in the technology sector ending in the third quarter of 2002, expecting a recovery that picks up speed in 2003. They see delayed expenditures and a healthier overall economy driving a 9.7 percent increase in IT investments in 2003, and 12 percent growth in the tech sector the following year.

Stepping back, it's interesting but not surprising that the media (and even some analysts) have framed the current unemployment rate as a "spike"—and the market for talent as loosening. At 5.6 percent,[4] current US unemployment is below the 6.0 percent rate that economists widely considered "full" employment for the span of the century through the mid-1990s.

In a study released this year, Watson Wyatt says, "Despite the slowing economy and layoffs, and despite the troubles facing certain industries, employers have not gained a significant advantage in attracting and retaining high-performance employees. There is no doubt that the labor shortage will continue, well into the next decade."[5]

Three-quarters of corporate officers surveyed by McKinsey & Co. last year agree, saying their companies are "chronically talent-short across the board," or suffer from "insufficient talent sometimes." Only 33 percent of 6,000 executives strongly agree that their companies attract highly talented people. Only 10 percent say they're successful at retaining high performers. Only three percent say their companies "actually develop their people quickly and effectively, or move low performers out quickly."[6]

What's more, the market will stay on the job seeker's side. Job creation, spurred largely by technology deployed across business sectors, is outpacing workforce growth. This country's demographic destiny is creating a net decline in the number of employed Americans, as baby boomers (born 1946–1964) start retiring in 2011. The Labor Department projects:

- From now until 2020, workforce growth will decline each year
- By 2008, we'll face a shortage of 10 million workers
- US companies will need to fill 55 million jobs over the next decade, but only 29 million potential employees will be available to take those jobs.[7]

But the bigger issue isn't quantity; it's quality—a situation compounded by a growing and increasingly critical skills gap. The half-life of skills is contracting, particularly in technology. The US Bureau of Labor Statistics (BLS) says through 2006, jobs requiring advanced degrees will grow at double the rate for all employment. A more complex economy is generating demand for more sophisticated talent at all levels.

As McKinsey & Co. put it, "Across the spectrum, the bar is being raised: the need is for executives with technological literacy, entrepreneurial skills, global acumen, ease in multi-cultural settings, and the ability to manage increasingly 'delayered,' disaggregated and

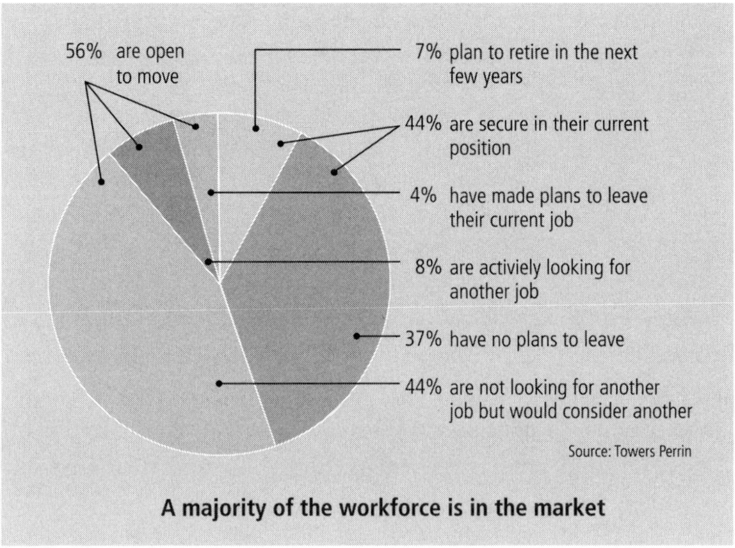

Figure 1. A majority of the workforce is in the market

networked organizations."[8] And on the assembly line, the shop floor, in the warehouse, traditional blue-collar jobs are requiring increasing levels of skill and comfort with information systems, cybernetic controls, and use of technology.

And, of course, the traditional employment "contract" of loyalty in exchange for lifetime employment melted in the 1980s and evaporated in the gold rush 1990s.

Right now, you can assume that over half of your people are open to moving on. According to a 2001 Towers Perrin survey of 6,000 US and Canadian employees, 56 percent of employees have made plans to leave, are actively looking, or are open to a move (see Figure 1).[9]

In that 2001, post-tech "meltdown" survey:

- 63 percent of all US workers and 75 percent of "fast track" performers are confident about their ability to find another job,

- 88 percent of managers indicated that finding and managing talent as much or more—not less—challenging than a year ago, and
- 92 percent of managers consider it as or more difficult to engage and motivate employees.

Present and potential employees have become much savvier "consumers," with better access to information about jobs, compensation, and employers-of-choice in their fields. The explosion of job boards and the ease of information distribution enabled by e-mail and the web have created a new class of what Towers Perrin calls "job scanners," continually evaluating their work options.[10] Candidates and employees with strong skills find themselves in particularly strong negotiating positions.

The Web is a Double-Edged Sword. Are You Holding the Right End?

Like any powerful tool, the Internet begets new challenges and begs new questions. Are we using the advantages of its distribution power effectively? Are oceans of un-navigable data and countless electronic résumé flat files the best possible thing to happen to the candidate and corporate experience—or the worst? And what should we do about it?

There has always been an inverse relationship between supply and demand—for anything, and particularly job candidates. You think

Present and potential employees have become much savvier "consumers," with better access to information about jobs, compensation, and employers-of-choice in their fields.

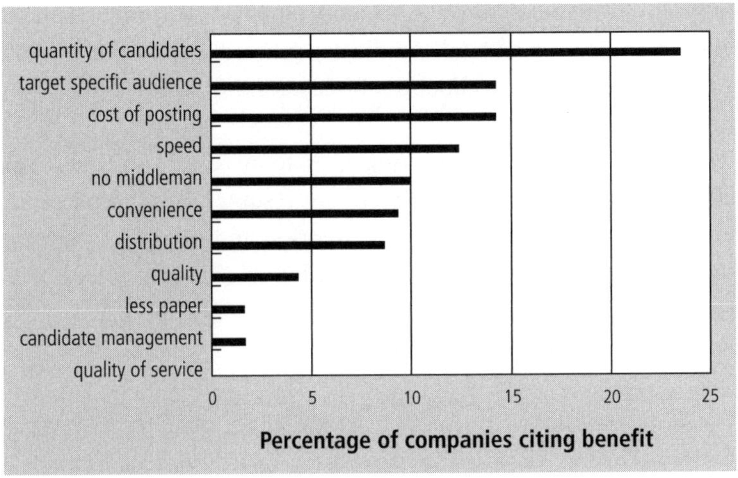

Figure 2. Web recruiting

you're either getting too many, or can't get enough. In fact, it's both: too many "irrelevant" ones, not enough "good" ones.

That has been exacerbated by the fact that the evolution of the web, as applied to recruiting in its mass-market incarnation, is still in its early Neanderthal stage. Job boards (and the companies that pay to post on them), applying the paradigms of the past, tend to regard the web as one big classified advertising section. As a result, the first-wave benefits of what most companies call "web recruiting" have been notably weak.[11]

The "greatest" virtue of e-recruiting—named by only 25 percent of respondents—has been *quantity* of candidates. And with duplicate response rates from the big mass-market job boards running at 40 percent, the volume those boards pitch as a "benefit" is, in fact, a seldom discussed but serious problem.

End-user benefits decline markedly after that. Only 13 percent of companies cite the ability to target specific audiences. Other studies indicate meager fill rates from large consumer job boards, despite huge investments of time, effort, and money. Companies average eight percent fill rates with candidates sourced on-line.[12] Last year we saw a 30 percent decline in job seeker satisfaction on-line.[13]

The current practice of posting jobs to massive consumer job boards and plowing through irrelevant résumés simply isn't good enough. "Despite the amount of attention and use of job boards, relatively few jobs may actually be initiated this way. Combined together, the top four job boards produced only about two percent of actual jobs for job hunters."[14]

Fortunately, some organizations are catching on. They're getting better at driving traffic to their own company's web destinations, delivering a better and more meaningful candidate experience, building direct relationships not mediated by mass-market job boards—and ultimately, building the company brand rather than paying the big job boards to develop theirs.

Since Forrester surveys indicate that by 2004, US corporations intend to increase their on-line spending 52 percent,[15] it will be all the more important for companies to get smarter about this—and get better tools and technology to do it.

There's a reason the first wave of e-recruiting under whelmed corporate America. The real value of the web isn't simply to enable universal distribution and bulk job postings. It's to enable one-to-one relationship building—and to drive enterprise workflow.

Talent Relationship Management (TRM)

Talent Relationship Management means developing talent as a strategic asset, in a broader and more constant sense, through every phase of the talent lifecycle—before people become candidates; while they're being recruited; after they've been hired. When they're considering their next move within the company (and before they're at risk of leaving); when they're corporate "alumni" that might refer or help close a key hire; always and all the time.

This is a tremendously collaborative set of activities. TRM can be practiced (and elements occasionally are) by companies of any size, but it is most critical and offers the biggest ROI for large, distributed organizations, particularly multinationals.

A definition:

> **tal.ent re.la.tion.ship man.age.ment (TRM)**: n (ca. 2001): **1 a:** the process and tools world-class organizations use to optimize the career experience they provide past, present, and potential employees; **b:** Applying best practices in database marketing and one-to-one communications to identify, cultivate, recruit, retain, and re-deploy people effectively; **2** Treating qualified candidates and motivated employees like preferred customers; **3** Competitive Advantage (**syn** see: CUSTOMER RELATIONSHIP MANAGEMENT, CRM)

To drive more precision and focus, a few things TRM *isn't*:

Talent Relationship Management is not "e-recruiting." Though best practices in e-recruiting are an important part of the picture, TRM extends across the employee lifecycle in ways e-recruiting doesn't. It doesn't simply apply "supply chain" principles to talent —the inventory model of human capital is profoundly limited, and applying technology to automate processes, clear transactions and eliminate paper is not the overriding goal of TRM, it's a basic pre-requisite.

Finally, it's important to emphasize that TRM is *not* about central planning—a few smart people behind desks using software to "plan" their way to the efficient allocation of human capital, aligned with strategic objectives and business unit requirements.

Though internal succession planning certainly has its place in large organizations, TRM means generating and sustaining an internal market efficiency well beyond the reach of a workforce planning tool that is only fully utilized by a few, because TRM relies on and enlists the interests, self interest, and engagement of the many—creating a dynamic, compelling market for talent within, across, and beyond the boundaries of the organization.

In that regard, TRM is more than an exercise in redistributive wisdom administered by an ERP or supply chain model, but it is the application of technology to harness something far more compelling, efficient, and effective: the power of the individual's sheer, glorious self-interest in the service of an organization's goals.

This may sound heretical to devotees of centralized supply chain models or workforce planning, but so did market capitalism to the Soviets. Anything as dynamic and complex as labor market demographics, changing employment relationships, and organizational performance is not amenable to a prescriptive, redistributed "solution." As you think about the potential implications of TRM for your company, think about developing and tapping the power of a *market* for talent within the organization, because the market will always be one step ahead of the planners.

The Power of Personalization

While TRM relies on the recruiting profession's longstanding reliance on person-to-person relationships, it uses technology to scale their reach and effectiveness. It can require substantial change management, to help an organization transform a passive, transactional hustle into a goal-driven process. And it demands that current employment relationships be personalized as well—continuing to analyze, segment, drive, and develop those relationships after an employee has signed on.

Recruiting	TRM
• Reactive	• Competitive
• Administrative (recruiters)	• Strategic (everyone)
• Transactional	• Collaborative
• Occasional	• Sustained
• Gate-keeping	• Gateways
• Just-in-time	• All-the-time
• Screening	• Fit
• One-way (filtering)	• Two-way (realtionships)
• Web = job boards	• Web = enterprise workflow
• Starts with new hires	• Starts with existing employees
• Fills jobs	• Drive business results

Figure 3. Recruiting and TRM

"Organizations," according to Towers Perrin, "are beginning to expect hiring managers, candidates, and employees to use web-enabled self-service recruiting tools as part of the reinvention of human resource departments. Organizations serious about TRM are training the entire enterprise in the process of treating candidates with respect and efficiency."[16]

That means understanding that while recruiting may once have been regarded as a function, TRM isn't a department (any more than CRM is)—it's an enterprise-wide *discipline* that extends to everyone in the organization. Figure 3 illustrates the differences between traditional recruiting and the evolutionary step forward represented by TRM.

Great recruiters, like great salespeople, do some of these things naturally. And under the right set of circumstances, more would. But getting serious about competing through talent means understanding that recruiters are the earliest link in the chain—

the front line or "inside sales" group an organization should use to qualify prospects—not the administrative department responsible for the outcome.

In the same way the discipline of CRM turned a disparate array of tools and functions into a coherent customer facing discipline, TRM makes the identification and development of talent a burning enterprise-wide priority. And because talent touches *every* aspect of organizational life, it is all the more complex—and all the more critical to get it right.

Five basic principles that inform the discipline of TRM:

1. **Recruitment, development, and redeployment are *one* continuous business process**, and must be managed that way. They're more costly and can never deliver the results you're looking for in isolation.

2. **The foundation of the process is a talent database that is cultivated and managed aggressively.** That means carefully cultivating and managing inbound data from all sources, live and on-line. Selective web assessment technologies and cycles of highly targeted outbound e-marketing campaigns qualify relationships. "High touch" through instant messaging (IM) and phone interactions are invested in qualified talent, turning the "digital stranger" experience into something that feels like a private community of highly qualified candidates with which the organization has (and has earned) relationships;

3. **This approach turns traditional recruiting on its head.** The old model was to advertise a job in the broadest medium and hope that the right candidates come to you. The new model shifts the paradigm from a job-seeker mentality (where the person had to find the right job) to a candidate-seeker mentality where the company takes the initiative to find the right candidate;

4. **Talent Relationship Management relies on good process management to be effective**, demanding thoughtful campaign design, careful execution, constant measurement, and analysis, obsessive elimination of bottlenecks, and clear feedback to (and accountability from) all of the players on the "buy" side. Refining that process yields a qualitatively superior employee and candidate experience; and

5. **When you generate enough superior employee and candidate experiences, you've put your organization on top of the supply/demand curve**—with the reward being access to broader and deeper talent pools, more motivated employees with clearer and more compelling career trajectories, products that ship on time, sales forecasts that materialize, and business units that run better, because the people behind them *are* better and are *doing* better.

Much of what makes this work, of course, is classic relationship marketing backed by substantial systems and technology—recognizing that both the employer brand and the employee value proposition need to be understood clearly, merchandized well, and differentiated clearly.

Building the Employer Brand

HR owns and builds a critical dimension of company brand—in the most substantive sense—as understood, felt, lived, and acted on every day, by the candidates and employees that make that company successful.

To do that, HR needs to draw on the disciplines of marketing—not just the piffle of marketing copy (though even that matters), but market segmentation, demographics, and database analysis, survey data, feedback, breaking down the problem, understanding the constituents, and factors driving perception—and getting the feedback back to line management which is the "R&D" (research and development), if you will, of the candidate and employee experience.

The employer brand shouldn't be something dreamed up by HR and marketing—it must be understood, supported and lived by the line management that interviews candidates and develops employees.

Don't Wait, Differentiate

A generally overlooked and underthought element here is meaningful differentiation of the employer brand, and the specific benefits that accrue to the individual (candidate or employee) should they decide to invest more time with you—on your employment website or in their career.

Once you've gotten and (to the degree possible) sustained the attention of a qualified "prospect"—and it's safe to assume doing so was quite costly—what are you doing with it and about it?

It's important to note that this doesn't just mean putting flashier graphics and cozier copy on the corporate website. Applying a now classic and proven approach used in marketing, it simply boils down to the unique selling proposition (USP), a concept that gained currency in the 1960s and has never lost its power.

In a nutshell:

- Make a proposition to the consumer. Not just words, not just product puffery, not just show-window advertising. Say to each reader: "Buy this product (*consider this job*), and you will get this specific benefit;" and
- The proposition must be one that the competition either cannot, or does not, offer. It must be unique—either a uniqueness of the brand or a claim not otherwise made in that particular field.[17]

Simply orienting the pitch away from job "qualifications" and toward the candidate/employee's interests, affinities, and priorities can make a tremendous difference.

This isn't as hard as it might sound. You can differentiate anything—as long as you offer customers more than they think they need, or have learned to expect.

The easiest way to do this is through continuing competitive due diligence. This seems like a given, but it is rarely used. The more time you spend reading your competitors' messaging, job descriptions, and postings on mass-market boards, the easier the problem appears. The vast majority present no clear value proposition to the candidate, fail to differentiate the offer, and instead deliver a very uncompelling recitation of job requirements layered with a few glowing generalities about growth and culture.

A day spent reading job classifieds, doing a careful analysis, and exegesis of the copy, is a tremendous education in how *not* to drive employment differentiation for current and potential talent—and is an important precursor to TRM.

Simply orienting the pitch away from job "qualifications" and toward the candidate/employee's interests, affinities, and priorities (it is, after all, about fit, which is never a one-way street) can make a tremendous difference.

A Pre-Flight Checklist for TRM

To begin framing out your tactical options and give shape to TRM, consider an array of potential tools and techniques:

I. Candidate & Employee Identification and Contact

- ✓ The corporate website should be the backbone of TRM. All advertising and promotions should drive traffic here. Carefully track traffic and results from job postings, banner ads on affinity sites, notices on targeted list servs, and bulletin boards, awareness ads, and newspaper advertising. Invest in tools that help you filter response volume productively.

- ✓ Once you've pulled a prospect to your site, simply presenting them with job listings will yield you no better than the average. Have you put at least as much energy and thinking into how you inform them, as what you want to learn about them?

- ✓ Avoid lengthy profile "builders" at all costs—to make the most of that web encounter, don't expect people to type their information in field-by-field. Make auto-extraction of electronic flat file résumé documents into relational data fields a requirement.

- ✓ Capture as much or as little information as the candidate/employee is willing to share on each encounter, giving them reasons to do so with each exchange. Don't expect to get without giving.

- ✓ As prospects indicate an inclination to respond, present qualitative and assessment questions *specific* to the job; it's easier than you think with the systems now available.

- ✓ Your system should score candidates and employees above defined thresholds set by managers when the position was opened. Whether you use a third party web assessment tool or develop questions yourself, workflow should enable higher-scoring candidates to be forwarded in real-time to the recruiter or hiring manager.

- ✓ All workflow to line managers should be driven through their e-mail client. Better systems launch fully-featured user interfaces (UIs) through direct authentication in e-mail, rather than requiring line managers to cope with yet another "manager's desktop." Expecting managers to log on to a software application to make TRM work is a losing proposition.

✓ Apply the same TRM design and workflow principles to your other sites. As necessary, deploy specialized destinations with workflow, content, business logic, branding, messaging, and a user experience *specifically* designed for your:

- Corporate intranet/employee jobsite
- College and university recruiting
- Employee referral programs
- Agency (headhunter) submissions, management, and tracking
- Corporate alumni board

Each of these sourcing channels will have distinct and specific expectations, and a world-class organization intent on generating the highest possible returns deploys process technology that works the problem at hand.

II. Building the Talent Record

✓ Candidates always want—and organizations always benefit by giving them—the freedom to share *as much* or *as little* information as they feel willing to share, *when they're ready to share it.* Arguments about whether the résumé is "dead" miss the point. Organizations serious about building relationships with talent deploy technology that extracts that data—in fully relational form—as a basis for building a much richer candidate profile. The résumé, whatever its source, form, or file format, is only the base currency of TRM. Don't just get over it—get beyond it.

✓ The résumé should be neither necessary nor sufficient. If the candidate/employee has a résumé, your system should support auto-extraction of its content, freeing their time to click the radio buttons and pull-downs that deliver the qualitative, qualifying information you need. If they don't have a résumé, be judicious in how much information you ask for early in the process. Ask for too much, and you won't get enough—particularly from more qualified candidates.

✓ Be sure your systems automatically create a *single* record from all sources, cross-checking and stacking duplicates automatically—unless your organization has time to confuse itself and prospects by duplicating efforts.

✓ Support the candidate/employee's ability to attach work samples and other documentation to their talent record and to deploy agents notifying them of upcoming positions, projects, or units that would benefit from their skills.

✓ Make sure the experience is at least as good as that delivered on the best consumer e-commerce destinations. You'd be surprised how far tools have come in this regard. Protect privacy, provide all of the information necessary, speak to their interests (not your requisitions), offer help, have an IM (instant message) option available (and staffed), and deliver an experience analogous to continuous world-class customer service. The better corporate jobsite destinations rival Amazon.com in their quality of user experience.

✓ A world-class TRM experience, for both candidates and employees, should feel familiar to them. If you've got any data

---

The goal of TRM is to develop a higher volume of meaningful interactions with fewer, more qualified prospects.

---

on them at all (and if you don't, what are they doing on your site to begin with?), the information presented and requested should feel like *their* turf, not yours. It should "feel like they know me," from the candidate/employee's perspective.

III. Building Relationships: Across the Talent Lifecycle

✓ Analyze the databases that get built as a result of the effort applied above. Enlist a couple of strong analysts from the marketing department, and have them start developing a meaningful market segmentation of your talent records, from both candidates and employees. Get their recommendations regarding the factors and attributes that account for your current traffic and response patterns—and ask them how they'd improve and refine the behavior set, based on your priorities.

✓ Using that segmentation, use the web to drive highly targeted "microcast" messages to the hard-to-hire segments most critical to your organization. Invoke the discipline of mass personalization, driving cycles of campaigns to specific targets with specific messages—using what you know in that database to market to them.

✓ At every step, as you drive those campaigns, provide helpful, relevant, meaningful, and interesting information. Don't start with a "job," any more than a salesperson builds a relationship by saying, "buy something." Base the messages on their professional interests and affinities.

✓ Messages must be relevant, well timed, helpful, and specific. Based on responses, continuously improve your ability to assess, analyze, and decide where to drive subsequent campaign cycles.

Rather than the high volume of *non* candidates the vast majority of organizations elicit through their current e-recruiting techniques, the goal of TRM is to develop a higher volume of meaningful interactions with *fewer*, more qualified prospects.

Deserving the attention, earning the confidence, and establishing the trust of jaded job seekers and employees takes time—and delivers much higher returns.

The Tools are Only Part of the Solution

It's a common mistake to attempt to make electronic communication a replacement for live interaction. Consider the web-based tool arsenal outlined above a "digital front door," *not* an endless corridor—necessary, important to be managed well, but not sufficient.

Use these tools to get to the right people faster, where you can and should invest the costly personal attention to pitch them and start building relationships with them by phone, IM, direct e-mail, or the medium of their choice.

Use your internal TRM systems as a support platform to make phone and live interaction more targeted and productive. Stop by your inside sales or phone-based customer support center, and look at their call center software and systems—that's what you should be aiming for here.

True Relationship Marketing: Building Great Networks

Studies indicate that, at the level of both the individual candidate and the market as a whole, no matter how much the volume of data (résumés and job postings) on the web grows, networking is still by far the most common way to locate a job.[18] What we all intuitively understand as "networking" is the individual doing relationship marketing. Essential to TRM is the understanding of how to leverage the power of networks to drive outcomes, and *institutionalize* relationship marketing.

An enterprise-level TRM system turns that fact to the organization's advantage, through on-line candidate referral tools, easy links to e-mail a job to a friend, and workflows and business logic that encourage (and reward) employees' engagement in the organization's continuing search for strong people.

Employee referral programs are often justified simply because of the lower cost—but they're supported by evidence that employee referrals are prequalified, have more relevant skill sets, have a better understanding of cultural and organizational fit up front, benefit from the trust built through their relationship with the referring employee, and have better retention rates.

TRM and the Talent Lifecycle

It's generally accepted that it's at least five times more profitable to retain an existing customer than to secure a new one. Now, apply the same metaphor to talent—and ask yourself if your organization devotes even a fraction of the attention to engaging and retaining employees that it does to recruiting them.

The talent lifecycle, properly understood, extends across the full spectrum of:

- Pre-candidacy
- Recruitment
- On-boarding
- First 90 days
- E-learning and development
- Performance appraisal and assessment

- Self-nomination/Internal candidacy
- Succession
- Referral sourcing
- Corporate alumni

But unlike customer retention and lifetime value, the question of employee retention and value is subtler. While a customer is a customer and a dollar is a dollar (where initial and repeat purchases are concerned), not all candidate interest and not all employee retention are good.

Amazon will sell a book to anyone who wants to buy it; you won't hire anyone who wants a job. Too many HR departments suggest that "people are our most important asset," but don't push further, helping line functions identify *which* people.

This speaks to the most critical dimensions of TRM—the *quality* of employee recruited and retained, the strength of the connection between their day-to-day work and overall company goals, and their degree of engagement with organizational success.

It is much harder to diagnose, never mind act on, employee engagement—but it's the ultimate driver of business success.

TRM provides a context to identify, manage and reward engagement. At a tactical level, it can be extremely effective to drive targeted e-mail newsletters and notices about new projects the company has won, new accounts ordeals that need motivated resources, new business units, new internal projects, new products, and new lines of business. And enterprise-wide, creating a dynamic internal market for talent is one of the most important things a large organization can do to become more competitive.

This may sound analogous to the "open book management" of the

1980s, but it has a much more pragmatic purpose and specific result: getting the right motivated people applied to the right business problems, and clearing the market for motivated talent effectively.

Too many HR departments suggest that "people are our most important asset," but don't push further, helping line functions identify which *people.*

The TRM Platform

Over the course of this decade (an eternity in software years), you will begin to see the evolution of true platforms for TRM that span the entire talent lifecycle. Out of the array of disconnected point solutions—and in distinct departure from the inevitable incrementalism of the large ERP vendors—the best-in class solutions will evolve to support a compelling coherence. Not because any of the vendors have a clue (though Lord knows we try), but because the market will demand it.

Customer relationship management as a discipline used to be incoherent, too—a disjointed range of solutions for marketing, sales force automation, service, and customer support—until businesses started looking at the entire customer life cycle, and focused on building and supporting relationships throughout that lifecycle, rather than simply automating activities.

In the same way, organizations are looking for ways to create meaningful connections between the major domains of human capital—recruitment, compensation, development, and appraisal. With the advent of XML and better integration tools, providers of best in-class solutions will assemble coherent, functional platforms, tightly integrated with the HRIS and ERP backend—and able to deliver far more configurable workflow, business logic that works the way actual people do, and faster time-to-value.

And as that happens, you'll see a much sought-after but little-understood outcome start to become a rational business expectation.

The Virtuous Cycle

Some companies generate a special set of circumstances—the highly-prized "virtuous cycle"; where a high-performing organization becomes an employer of choice, and is able to attract, engage and retain outstanding employees whose work further strengthens the company, creating an even more high performing organization.

It's difficult, to be sure, but it's really not that complicated.

In the coming years we're going to see the introduction of far more sophisticated systems for assessment, performance support technology, and e-learning that enable motivated employees to continue to develop, give companies much sharper insight into their key competitive asset, and link back to that dynamic internal market for talent described earlier.

Such systems will make it easier to create a real value proposition for employees. That employee value proposition will be far more personalized—reflecting the employees' knowledge, skills, abilities, interests, and affinities—and focused on outcomes and results delivered, rather than programs and dollars administered, as too many one-to-many training programs have been.

And as those systems get linked and integrated with the "front-end" of the talent management process, the employee lifecycle will start to acquire the same coherence that the customer lifecycle did in the last decade.

An organization that practices TRM acts on the fact that employee "loyalty" is not about preserving the status quo or a static working relationship—it's about the way the employment relationship, like any relationship, will (and must) evolve over time to remain vital. In an organization, for the employment relationship to be meaningful, it must be personalized.

Evolving the Employee Lifecycle: Factors that Drive Engagement

The market for information being what it is on the web and around the water-cooler, any messaging in excess of reality will be quickly identified for what it is, and punished in the marketplace.

As the Talent Market Group notes, "Companies must communicate an accurate and consistent employer-of-choice message. Quality candidates require employers to identify and quantify the reasons that they deserve their skills, time, and talent. They demand employers match their message with the actual work experience."[19]

The key to this—just as it was with the candidate experience—is personalization:

- **Analyze talent—do the market research.** Understand the asset your employees represent, and break the problem down. Gather reliable data from employees—not just employee satisfaction surveys (though those matter), but also substantive surveys of their take on the business and marketplace as well as data about them (demographics, skills, affinities, interests, perceptions, needs).

  Understand what they value at different stages of their careers. The priorities, skills, interests, and affinities of Gen-X entrants versus mid-career balancers versus senior managers are a matrix you need to understand—connect with—and sell to. And it's a moving target; you have to keep revisiting, and recalibrating.

- **Keep up-selling the experience.** Know what you have to offer beyond the common denominators of retention (pay and benefits), and how they appeal to different segments of your candidate and employee population—particularly the high performers that you want to keep. And keep reselling it to them. Merchandise the employment contract or "deal" you want existing and potential employees to have with your organization.

  The "deal" a company makes with its people is of course many deals that need to evolve over time as business needs and employees' mix of priorities changes. Assume your competitors are pitching your strong contributors constantly. This matters as much in hard economic times as it does in good economic times to drive employee engagement.

- **Recruit high performers and people with hard-to-replace skill sets continually.** This isn't as hard as it sounds. Hosting web destinations with opportunities to advance, driving targeted internal e-mail campaigns, getting information out about new projects, and initiatives that enlist employees directly can be very powerful.

- **Make the bigger picture go "click" in talent's mind.** Drive clear communications that enable employees to see the connection between their work and larger company objectives—the "so what" of what they do every day. The degree to which your people understand what drives customer and market value, and have a clear and compelling thread in their minds between what they do and financial results, is a critical driver of alignment, engagement, and performance. Managers need guidance in tying meaningful (and not just monetary) rewards to employees delivering on those larger goals.

- **Reinforce retention—selectively.** Universal retention without regard for performance and potential, of course, is neither possible nor desirable—and tends to demoralize stronger employees. A better approach uses highly targeted efforts aimed at particular individuals, including creative compensation, job customization, and strengthening employees' social ties to teammates.[20]

Cracking the Internal Talent Paradox

Underlying all this, there is a paradox at work in most organizations that can be a real impediment to successful TRM—and needs to be managed deliberately and directly. On the one hand, employees want to advance to another stage. They need to connect with other opportunities in the organization, and be able to self-nominate and drive their own career development.

Too many managers, on the other hand, regard their interest as keeping those employees contributing right where they are—productive, static, and ultimately unhappy. Managers tend to reinforce the (false) perception of a zero sum talent game with each other by "poaching" stronger members of each other's teams without communicating directly with the other "side's" manager—making talent something traded on the black market, as employees seek surreptitious meetings with managers they hope will help them advance.

One option is to make a talent development objective an explicit part of the goals managers are compensated on. Creating a management bonus component for the number of people promoted out from *under* managers might sound unusual—but might help.

Another way to un-glue this paradox is to create transparent, reasonable business rules through systems that encourage early and better communication between managers, and create an open and efficient market.

Enlightening some managers to the inspired self-interest of their people's advancement within the larger organization may not sound easy—but consider the humble fax machine's role in driving *glasnost* in the Soviet Union and the democratic impulse in China. Web TRM systems create an open market for talent, breaking open the paradox of internal market, and creating a context for business rules, communication, process, transparency, and trust.

If You're Restructuring or Downsizing—TRM is More Critical, Not Less

Another paradox, borne of the "inventory" view of talent, is the myth that TRM doesn't matter in a downturn. Nothing could be further from the truth.

Announcements of mass layoffs aren't simply devastating to the affected employees. They seriously compromise the confidence of those that remain—not to mention all that has been invested, in practice and in brand, to develop and support the company's reputation as an employer of choice. And there search shows across-the-board layoffs rarely generate the cost savings expected in the short run, and almost always compromise competitiveness. Across-the-board cuts, early retirement, and departure packages have taken a heavy toll on company strength and long-term performance.[21]

TRM provides an important opportunity for companies to do a better job managing the inevitable swings, restructurings, and the need to accommodate the business cycle that will never quite go away.

By creating meaningful links and feedback loops between performance assessment systems, skills analysis, and business requirements—and driving more robust workforce analytics—TRM technology provides an opportunity for more surgical, strategic changes that strengthen an organization, using performance as a guide.

Fully 73 percent of companies continue to hire talented employees in the midst of downsizing, and nearly half have created targeted programs to retain top performers.[22] TRM provides a solution to these cycles, helping companies hire more selectively, develop more actively, cultivate the employment relationship more deliberately, and make hard decisions based on individual performance data, interests and aptitudes, rather than across-the-board.

Mass layoffs are the human equivalent of "blowing out" inventory at below cost—except the "inventory" walks out with the institutional and process knowledge, customer relationships, skills, and experience that help the company compete. An organization that practices TRM knows better.

Contract and Contingent Talent

While it's outside the scope of this article, there's a clear need to integrate an organization's management of full-time talent with its use of contractors and contingent workforce.

To date, even at world-class organizations, full-time and contract talent are still procured in silos—HR "owns" the FTE process, and procurement or IT "owns" contractors and the vendor management systems used to clear transactions with contract staffing firms.

Over the next few years, since managers ultimately should initiate a requisition thinking clearly about the trade-offs between using contractors versus hiring full-time staff—and organizations should have enterprise-wide visibility into the cost-effectiveness of both approaches, not to mention more rational temp-to-permanent transitions—you can expect to start seeing connections between systems for managing FTE talent and those used to procure contractors.

TRM Drives Higher Shareholder Returns

Many companies have reported 100 percent return on investment for HR self service-products as a result of reduced head count, transaction costs, and cycletime.[23] Leading-edge TRM solutions are enabling Fortune 500 firms to save as much as US $10 million to US $15 million per year in actual hard costs in some cases—savings associated with process improvement around recruitment and reducing fees paid to third parties.[24]

But as argued above, making the case based on cost savings is only part of the story. There's a much bigger point to be made.

If you're still wondering whether TRM will resonate in the executive suite, Towers Perrin's research shows that high performing organizations—as defined by five-year total shareholder return for publicly traded companies—are rated more highly by employees on the dimensions that TRM addresses directly. Individuals gain the highest levels of employment satisfaction in environments where their talents and skills are most productively put to use.

For high-performing organizations, according to Towers Perrin:

- 72 percent of employees rate their company as a good employer (versus 52 percent on average)
- 38 percent of employees rate their company well for developing leaders in the organization (versus 27 percent on average)
- 32 percent of employees rate their company as fully tapping into their skills and abilities (versus 22 percent on average).

High-performing companies are able to engage employees in their business—and that is reflected in total shareholder returns that are 10 points higher than the S&P 500 average.[25] There is a clear link between TRM and financial performance.

Other research supports this. "Superior human capital practices are not only correlated with financial returns, they are, in fact, a *leading* indicator of increased shareholder value. Superior HR

High-performing companies are able to engage employees in their business—and that is reflected in total shareholder returns that are 10 points higher than the S&P 500 average. There is a clear link between TRM and financial performance.

practices are a key to attraction, retention, and, more and more, business outcomes."[26]

While there's a reasonable link (correlation .19, according to Watson Wyatt's studies) between companies' positive financial results and better human capital practices (logical enough—wealthier companies fund better programs)—there's much *stronger* correlation (.41) between better human capital practices and financial return.

In other words: Good human capital management practices aren't simply associated with good business outcomes—*they create them.*[27]

In a seminal book published in 2000, Jac Fitz-enz of the Saratoga Institute argued that "the focus on the interaction between human capital and financial outcomes is a leading rather than a coincidental reason for their long-term financial success."

"The belief in people at a financial level is extremely rare," he says. "I struggle for words of sufficient power to cause you to stop and contemplate this. No matter what the public relations department puts out about people being important, on a daily basis in the executive aerie, people are considered to be an expense . . . beyond the sales function [where an incremental sales head can drive incremental revenue], executives don't have the slightest inkling of how to tie human effort directly to financial results."[28]

TRM provides a framework, a process, and information technology to do precisely that: tying the quality of people recruited, the employer brand, their engagement as employees, their development and performance to organizational and financial outcomes.

Conclusion

In the classic hierarchy of the "modern" corporation, investors come first . . . then customers . . . then employees. Perhaps in the post-Enron era, those three elements will warrant something approaching equal attention, and come to be seen to be as interdependent as they truly are.

While the musings of Karl Marx have been discredited by the triumph of market-oriented capitalism, he did get a singular point right, about the primacy of human capital. But ultimately, managing talent effectively in the current market is less an argument of ethics, central planning, social equity, or redistributive integrity, as it is a matter of sheer competitive self-interest.

We competed on quality in the 1970s, time in the 1980s, and information systems in the 1990s. In this decade, we will take on the last critical dimension of competitive advantage: We will learn to compete through talent. Not just "for" talent—*through* talent.

Talent is the last, most difficult, and most indispensable element of competitive advantage. It is the only problem—and the one opportunity—that won't go away.

Endnotes

1 U.S. Department of Labor/Bureau of Labor Statistics: National Compensation Survey, 2000.

2 BLS January 2002; Institute for Retail Excellence; Baird, 2001 HR Partnership Summit.

3 Gartner/Dataquest estimates, 2001.

4 As of this writing, the Bureau of Labor Statistics/U.S. Department of Labor puts the January 2002 seasonally adjusted unemployment rate at 5.6 percent.

5 Watson Wyatt, *Human Capital Index Survey Report*: "Human Capital as a Lead Indicator of Shareholder Value," 2001/2002.

6 Ed Michaels, Helen Handfield-Jones, and Beth Axelrod, *The War for Talent*, (Boston: Harvard Business School Press, 2001).

7 The Towers Perrin Talent Report 2001: *New Realities in Today's Workforce*; U.S. Bureau of Labor Statistics.

8 *The War for Talent.*

9 Towers Perrin.

10 The Economist Intelligence Unit and Towers Perrin: *Business, People and Rewards:Surviving and Thriving in the New Economy*, 2001.

11 Hunt Scanlon, 1999.

12 Employment Management Association.

13 Weddle's Annual Survey.

14 K. Maher, R.E. Silverman, cited by F.Lievens and M. Harris in "Research on Internet Recruitment and Testing,"Ghent University and U. Missouri, January 2002.

15 Forrester Research; Baird.

16 Towers Perrin.

17 Rosser Reeves, *Reality in Advertising*, (New York: Knopf, 1960), pp. 47-48.

18 Lievens & Harris.

19 John Chaisson and Connie Pascal, *Top Ten Challenges of Corporate Recruiting 2001: Emergence of the Talent Management Organization*, Talent Market Group, Inc., 2001.

20 Peter Capelli, "A Market-Driven Approach to Retaining Talent," *Harvard Business Review*, January-February 2000.

21 Towers Perrin.

22 Towers Perrin.

23 Britton Manasco, William S. Hopkins, and Lewis J. Perelman, "Human Capital Management Solutions: Capitalizing on the New Technologies of Recruitment, Learning and Workforce Management," Knowledge Capital Group, 2001.

24 *Ibid.*

25 Towers Perrin.

26 Watson Wyatt.

27 *Ibid.*

28 Jac Fitz-enz, *The ROI of Human Capital: Measuring the Economic Value of Employee Performance*, (New York: American Management Association, 2000).

> “We are what we repeatedly do. Excellence, then is not an act, but a habit.”

—Aristotle

1

The Corporate ROI of Direct Contractor Engagement

MATTHEW BENDER AND AUSTIN WHITMAN

Matthew Bender is the Director of Corporate Communications for Contractors Resources, Inc. A ten-year veteran in the technology and workforce communications arena, Mr. Bender has penned articles for over a dozen national publications and has written content for nearly thirty websites. Mr. Bender received his BA in English from James Madison University and he can be reached at mbender@contractorsresources.com.

Austin Whitman brings experience in writing and analysis to BrassRing where he focuses on helping to position the company's growth and strategy in the marketplace. Before joining BrassRing he was an online content manager for a successful educational start-up in Silicon Valley. He holds a BA in English from Dartmouth College and can be reached at awhitman@brassring.com.

The continuous flow of information across the Internet has demystified contract talent sourcing. Staffing firms are losing the advantage they once held over corporate recruiters whose roles are growing more strategic as they drive down sourcing costs by leveraging a variety of on-line recruiting tools. By applying successful full-time recruitment and retention strategies to the direct procurement and employment of contractors, companies can shave millions of dollars from their contract spend and bridge one of the more costly extant gaps in human capital management: the HR/Procurement divide.

Before the Internet's debut as a recruiting tool, staffing suppliers were able to dominate the market for contract talent. Suppliers held inherent advantages in connecting talent with opportunities because they could aggregate jobs and individuals and market them both in a single storefront. Companies had little choice but to go through suppliers to find contractors, who in turn relied on the same suppliers for job opportunities.

Efficiencies have started to take hold in an Internet-enabled world. Corporations have been deploying Talent Relationship Management (TRM) platforms to build talent pools, foster relationships with current and potential employees, and build process efficiencies. When applied to contract staffing, TRM principles help companies actualize many of the same benefits.

A key piece of the puzzle is held by a new category of vendor, Contract Employment Services Providers (CESPs), which enable companies to outsource the main administrative nightmare—managing the engagement of contractors—that is traditionally overseen by the staffing provider. This allows companies to keep the recruitment of contractors in house, free of staffing firm costs.

As a result of both TRM and CESPs, the direct recruitment and engagement of contractors has grown into a realistic option for employers, who stand to benefit from:

- **Procurement cost savings.** Companies no longer pay excessive fees (in the form of hourly rate markups) to procure contract labor.
- **Bridging the corporate divide.** In most companies, HR owns FTE hiring and the Procurement function owns relationships with staffing vendors and the process for managing contract labor.[1] Procurement applies a supply-chain mentality to talent acquisition, while HR has little input and few responsibilities. Organizations are beginning to bridge the chasm between Procurement and HR by leveraging their TRM platforms to engage contract talent directly, saving millions of dollars and increasing quality control in the management of the contingent workforce.
- **Consistent selection.** One of the greatest ironies of contingent talent procurement today is companies tend to utilize less demanding selection methods for contract employees, even though they often work on some of the most critical projects. Companies could benefit by implementing more unified selection practices across all categories of talent.

- **Preservation of knowledge.** Contractors gain a tremendous amount of institutional knowledge about your company during an engagement. When they leave, they take that knowledge along with them. Meanwhile, you possess valuable knowledge about each contractor's performance. Under the current market model, this information vanishes at the close of the contract engagement. Building and maintaining your own relationships with contractors can help preserve this knowledge for future use.

This paper provides a background on the contract labor market and covers some of the reasons why organizations have favored contract talent in recent years. It explains the cost of using agencies in sourcing contingent talent. And it shows that some essential principles and best practices in Talent Relationship Management can lead to dramatic cost savings in contingent hiring by cutting out the intermediary staffing company.

Contract Staffing in the Pre-Internet Era

The contractor work style has become indispensable in recent decades because of its benefits to both employers and contractors. In the classic model of contract staffing, companies procure contractors through contract staffing providers because those providers have better access to talent.

The Shift from The Lifetime Employment Standard

Over the last quarter century corporations have begun to embrace a new class of employee. During the downsizing periods of the 1980s an erosion of loyalty throughout the workforce drove a cultural shift away from the standard of lifetime employment. In addition, rapid technological progress at the end of the 20th century forced established businesses to become more agile. Companies repeatedly re-evaluated and overhauled their core workforce competencies to keep pace with changing business needs. Contracted professionals, commonly known as consultants, freelancers, independents, flexible workers, or alternative workers,

Advantages of Contract Engagements

Companies engaging contractors to fill specialized roles have realized that the advantages of using contractors extend beyond the skills and knowledge they bring to their work assignments. The inherent non-permanence of these workers means reduced overhead costs and easier severability. Companies can leverage contractors to add new capabilities quickly without having to retrain their core staff. They can bring on independent talent for a period of months or even weeks, then disengage with them when their contracted work is complete.

Companies can maximize their utilization by aligning labor capacity more closely to demand. CFOs commonly favor use of a contingent workforce, as they can leverage contractor engagements to shift Human Capital Management expenditures from 100 percent fixed costs to a higher percentage of variable costs.

As a result, contractor engagements have become popular and widespread throughout all industries, departments, and job functions. A McKinsey & Company report suggests that as much as 15 to 25 percent of large companies' workforce is non-permanentC1. This popularity does not appear to be letting up: by 2004 the majority of $1 billion + companies are expected to use contactors for more than half of their IT positions.[C2]

Companies, it is important to note, aren't the only ones benefiting from contract arrangements. Job satisfaction soars among contractors, with 83 percemt of independent contractors preferring the 'independent' work style.[C3] Not only can they work when and where they want on projects of their own choosing; they can generally make more money and take more time off than they can in a traditional corporate environment.

C1—McKinsey & Company, 2000 • C2—Gartner, 2001 • C3—US Bureau of Labor Statistics, 2001

fit both the new behavioral preferences of workers and the revolving demand for technical skill sets.

Contractors possess specialized, leading-edge skills and can quickly convey executive vision into workable solutions. Their skills, not their companies, define their careers. Given the benefits it offers to both the contractor and the employer, the contract engagement model has become a mainstay of employment in most economies around the world. (*See boxed text above.*)

Staffing Suppliers Meet New Demand

The evolution of the contract worker stimulated the growth of a new industry: contract staffing services providers. Staffing providers fulfill two critical functions for clients seeking to bring on contract talent: *recruitment* and *employment*. Staffing providers first receive contract requisitions from their client companies and recruit appropriate candidates for the open positions. Then, after the client selects a contractor, the staffing provider serves as the contractor's official "employer of record," delivering employment-related services such as payroll, health benefits, retirement programs, tax management, and so forth.

Staffing firms—and, to an even greater degree, major consulting companies—"bundle" their recruitment and employment services into a single rate (billing rate) that represents a mark-up from the actual hourly amount the contractor earns (pay rate). This mark-up ranges anywhere from 35 to 200 percent, depending on various factors and negotiations between the parties. In most cases, staffing providers don't disclose the components of their rate structure, which safeguards their ability to set their billing rate at whatever level the market will bear, almost regardless of the contractor's pay rate.

Contract Staffing Suppliers—the Dominant Model

Despite such high markups, companies needing contractors continue to rely heavily on a multitude of staffing providers (over 5,000 to be precise). The staffing industry now represents well over $66 billion[2] in contractor billings—a figure that doesn't include related companies such as consulting firms and other outsourced functions. Staffing providers have become the *de facto* contract talent engagement channel and their core model has remained remarkably unchanged. Hiring companies have been using the same tactics to acquire contract talent through third party suppliers for nearly thirty years.

Contract Staffing in the Internet Era

Having reviewed the history and value of the contract model of employment, we turn now to a discussion of the way the Internet has altered the dynamic between employers and contractors by removing the inherent advantages once possessed by staffing providers. Leading companies are now able to recruit and engage contractors directly.

The Internet and Disintermediation of the Staffing Firm

In recent years "recruiting" has become synonymous with "e-recruiting." The Internet has had tremendous influence on the FTE recruiting activities of companies, becoming an indispensable tool for accessing talent pools in every imaginable arena: job boards, on-line communities, personal home pages, listservs, newsgroups, corporate websites, intranets, and so on. In less than a decade, the Internet has taken a significant chunk out of the total number of dollars companies spend on recruitment advertising in printed media. Every major company enlists the Internet at some point in its routine FTE hiring cycles.

Though transparent to client companies, the Internet has also driven a sea change in the way *staffing providers* recruit *contractors*. While staffing firms still build and maintain their own talent databases, a significant portion of their recruitment activities is dedicated to straightforward searches of public Internet databases. That's why it's quite common—and hardly coincidental– for multiple staffing providers to submit the same résumé for a given req.

So how has the Internet changed contract talent procurement for the employer? Recognizing the tremendous process inefficiencies inherent in placing contractor orders with multiple staffing companies at once, a category of ASPs known as Vendor Management Systems (VMSs) has arisen. They act as intermediaries between the client and staffing firms. Their software consolidates orders and billing for multiple contractors and multiple providers over the web.

Yet the real value of the Internet isn't simply to enable bulk submissions of job orders to staffing companies. Instead, the Internet enables one-to-one relationship building with all types of talent, and the resultant cost savings brought on because you can "do it yourself." Staffing companies no longer have an advantage when it comes to finding contractors. In the current evolutionary phase, employers are learning to disintermediate contract staffing suppliers by attracting and engaging contractors directly.

The Direct Engagement Model for Contractors

As noted earlier, staffing firms provide value in two main areas: *recruitment* of contractors and managing the employment engagement. As long as employers believe they cannot replicate these functions cheaply in house, the staffing supplier model remains viable. Indeed, until recently direct contractor engagement was riddled with inefficiency.

Some classic obstacles to direct engagement have included:

- **Recruiting challenges.** Most companies simply aren't equipped to recruit contractors. Contractor procurement is almost always performed at the Project Manager level; despite their recruiting proficiency, HR departments rarely get involved with contract workers.
- **Administrative challenges.** Even when a company is successful in finding appropriate contractors independently, each contractor then works as a separate vendor to the company. The administration of this can be tedious, expensive, and error-prone.
- **Legal challenges.** Direct contractor engagements can carry risks. IRS and labor law officials can force hiring companies to reclassify their independent contractors (those not working as a W-2 to any company) as full-time employees. As the world witnessed with such companies as Microsoft and

TimeWarner, the associated tax implications, back-benefits payments, and punitive costs can be staggering.

- **Tax assessment challenges.** Until 1986, when the IRS issued Section 1706 to officially define and differentiate contract workers from full-time employees, tax requirements surrounding contract workers were vague. Before then, the IRS wasn't even collecting standard payroll taxes (such as Social Security and income taxes) from contract workers.

At first glance, the ability to recruit contractors directly may not appear to translate into significant cost savings. Even if a client recruits a contractor on its own, it must still turn to a staffing provider to employ the contractor and handle administrative services.

A new class of service providers, known as Contractor Employment Services Providers (CESPs) has emerged with an inexpensive option for companies that locate talent on their own. CESPs "unbundle" the previously indivisible staffing functions by offering standalone contractor *employment* services. CESPs provide top-tier benefits, employment administration (payroll, taxes, etc.), and other employment-related programs, thereby offering a cost-effective alternative for businesses that locate talent on their own.

Corporations Invest in TRM Platforms for Full-Time Hiring

For the Direct Contractor Engagement (DCE) alternative to succeed, companies must extend their existing recruitment processes to displace the recruitment normally provided by staffing firms. Companies have been investing in Talent Relationship Management (TRM) platforms to improve their core FTE recruitment and management functions. As you'll see, TRM provides a powerful strategy for recruiting more effectively than the staffing firm.

Talent Relationship Management is an approach that empowers

CESPs and the Individual Contractor

The direct contractor engagement concept is made possible by an employment model introduced during the 1980s.

Contractor Employment Services Providers (CESPs) serve as "portable employers" for contract workers. Participants become W-2 employees of the CESP, thereby enjoying the most convenient tax status possible, yet they retain the freedom of independent professionals. They obtain their own contracts and set their own rates, while retaining their CESP as their employer across all projects.

As W-2 employees of a large organization, the contractors have access to corporate-style group-rate benefits (health insurance, retirement programs, etc.) and are relieved of the burden of quarterly tax filings. The CESP also performs administrative functions such as client billing, collections, and paycheck distribution. And the CESP offers a unique pre-tax expense reimbursement program that commonly saves members thousands of tax dollars each year.

The CESP model offers convenient services to members, coupled with potential cost savings for employers. Members work only when and where they want, on projects of their own choosing. The result is a powerful combination that is attractive to both sides.

organizations to drive competitive advantage through talent by optimizing engagements with *past, present*, and *potential* employees.

TRM means engaging in the continuous pursuit and development of talent throughout the entire talent lifecycle and applies to every class of talent: full-time, contingent, part-time, and hourly.

Practitioners of TRM understand that it requires a continuous approach and patient focus on building rich pools of talent. They understand that TRM relies on the existence of—and the ongoing effort to build—a reliable repository of talent data that is accessible to the entire organization. This repository ("talent pool") serves as a strategic asset—a talent reserve accessible on demand.

Companies are realizing that TRM methods, when extended to

contract recruitment, provide a sustainable, cost-effective alternative to the recruitment services offered by staffing firms. A dedicated internal recruiter with a TRM focus and access to the most popular on-line job boards and contractor marketplaces can produce the same results as a typical staffing recruiter. Later in this paper, we'll suggest some best practices in TRM for engaging contractors.

ROI: Save Millions by Dodging Staffing Markups

By recruiting contractors internally and employing them through a CESP, clients can reduce their overall mark-up by between 50 and 70 percent. For example, companies that once paid their staffing providers a billing rate of $100/hour for a contractor with a $70/hour pay rate (a 43 percent mark-up) can now pay about $82/hour (a 17 percent mark-up) by recruiting internally and using a CESP for all contractor employment services. The resulting $18/hour difference translates into an annual savings of over $35,000—for just one contractor.

Just as importantly, the costs savings here do not necessitate a decrease in the quality of talent. This example represents rates for *the same contractor* serviced through different models.

This savings model has extraordinary ramifications. The table below shows the total contractor expenditures of a typical large company using 500 contractors,[3] as well as how much it would

Current overall cost using staffing providers	**$56,880,000**			
% of client's contractor workforce engaged directly using CESP	**10%**	**33%**	**70%**	**100%**
Overall cost using a CESP for all directly engaged contractors	**$55,825,759**	**$53,401,003**	**$49,500,310**	**$46,337,586**
Potential savings using a CESP & engaging contractors directly	**$1,054,241**	**$3,478,997**	**$7,379,690**	**$10,542,414**

have saved if it had engaged various percentages of its contractor workforce directly using a CESP.

As you can see from this example, clients can expect to save over $1 million for every fifty contractors they recruit on their own and engage through a CESP.

It is important to understand that this model can be extremely effective without completely supplanting your relationships and transactions with staffing suppliers. You may find that 60 percent of your contractors can be readily sourced without help from a staffing company, but that the remaining 40 percent require the assistance of a third party supplier—and that's fine. The key thing is that you begin to drive cost savings by leveraging the direct engagement approach to the extent it makes sense in your organization.

Direct Contractor Engagement: Other Advantages

While the tremendous cost savings potential is the primary driving force behind the escalating adoption of the direct contractor engagement approach, it produces other advantages as well.

- **Free and convenient Master Agreement.** Your relationship with a CESP usually takes the form of a Master Services Agreement. This single agreement covers the terms and conditions for all contractors engaged through the CESP and there is generally no charge for the establishment of this agreement.
- **Consolidated billing.** CESPs consolidate all of their contractors at a given client on a single invoice. This alleviates your administrative overhead and reduces payment errors.
- **More satisfied workforce.** Because CESPs focus exclusively on understanding and serving the unique needs of the contract workforce, these workers tend to be more satisfied with their employment situation.

- **Solution complements existing processes.** When using a CESP to engage internally-recruited contractors, you can employ as few or as many contractors as you wish. In this way, CESPs don't require abandonment of your current staffing providers (which you may still tap for harder-to-fill positions) but rather serve as an attractive alternative.
- **Permanent relationships.** By engaging contractors directly you have permanent direct access to them and may re-engage with them at any time without paying fees to staffing providers.
- **Improved consistency in selection.** By utilizing the same recruiting staff for the procurement and selection of contractors that you do for your full-time workforce, you'll have greater success enforcing consistent selection practices. Corporate culture and values will factor more powerfully in selection decisions.

Applying TRM Best Practices to Contract Staffing

As we've illustrated, direct contractor engagement can bear significant advantages for your organization. We'll now discuss some best practices in TRM that can enhance your ability to implement a direct contractor engagement approach.

TRM Principles Foster Productivity in the DCE Model

Communicating with prospective contractors in messages that are personalized, relevant, and targeted brings significant sustainable advantages to companies. A quick return to Talent Relationship Management fundamentals shows that a TRM approach extends neatly to the process of direct contractor engagement.

- **The relationship is the keystone of business success.** TRM enables companies to engage talent more cost-efficiently and derive more value over time as a result of strong relationships. Consider that with good relationships, you will find yourself re-engaging with contractors again and again. Rather than wasting cycles hunting for inexperienced contractors through staffing companies, you'll be fishing from pools of experienced contractors who know about your business, and on whom you already have significant data.

- **TRM focuses on the entire lifecycle of the employee, from initial contact through separation.** Companies practicing TRM recognize the value that past employees can add to an organization. Former contractors can provide value to you in the form of employee referrals, new business, or another productive contract engagement.

- **Companies' recruiting efforts should be sustained continuously in all economic climates.** Companies have historically relied on contractors in both strong and weak economies. In every climate it's important to have quick, cost-efficient access to contract talent. TRM helps build talent pools for this very purpose.

- **TRM systems provide enterprise-wide visibility.** Organizations that deploy technology to support TRM do so with an eye toward unifying business process, workflows, data stores, and analytics across the entire company. You will not get a handle on contract staffing expenses if staffing continues to happen at a local level funded with multiple discretionary, hard-to-track budgets. A TRM platform eliminates confusion over how dollars are being allocated and helps eliminate phantom expenses.

- **TRM is about keeping rich data and delivering reports on demand.** With a TRM platform in place to manage direct contractor engagements, you can analyze your contract staffing activity and deliver accurate reports on expenditures, recruiter productivity, database content, and many other metrics. You'll gain tremendous insight from the ability to compare your full-time and contract hiring activities on a single TRM platform.

- **TRM helps refine talent sourcing.** As a source of talent, staffing companies provide a quick fix but little insight over the long run. You may learn which staffing companies serve you best, but you won't learn why. Controlling the sourcing process in-house will allow you to gather data over time and learn what works and what doesn't. You'll also learn to correlate full-time and contract sourcing effectiveness. If your best full-time employees all come from a single source, wouldn't it be wise to return to the same pond when it comes time to fish for contractors?

Some Keys to Driving Contractor Engagement

In order to benefit from direct engagement of contractors, you'll need to refine your marketing messages targeted at contractors. They have different expectations from the full-time class of talent and as a result they'll react to different value points. Following are some suggestions for tailoring your recruitment messages to your audience and deploying tools to facilitate the direct engagement:

- **Build a strong Employee Value Proposition for contractors.** An Employee Value Proposition (EVP) comprises the reasons why your organization is an attractive place to work.[4] Will staffing providers help you refine your EVP? Not likely. They are there to meet demand, on demand. The finer points are lost, not because they don't matter but because your supplier's account rep has already moved on to filling the next order. By building a strong EVP, you will attract the types of contractors with the greatest potential to fit right into your organization—the ones who will have the greatest impact on your success.

- **Market a larger opportunity**. According to Towers Perrin, an effective way of attracting talent is to figure out a position that will serve as an "entry point" into your organization.[5] When possible, advertise contract openings in ways that suggest there is life beyond the end of the contract—perhaps in another contract engagement, perhaps as a full-time employee.

- **Deploy a specialized web front-end.** Create a destination website with workflows and opportunities specifically geared toward your audience of potential contractors. Make sure it captures as the information you need without asking for too much. By driving traffic to an on-line website you'll be able to leverage existing web-based screening and assessment tools, asking questions specific to each opportunity. The website should be integrated with your TRM platform.

- **Market your opportunities as the "next best thing" for candidates.** Think back to the discussion of contract employment earlier in this paper. Contractors have different objectives from full-time candidates. Your opportunity needs to make sense for their professional development over the short term. When they're out looking for another engagement in six months, how will your engagement have made them more marketable?

- **Understand the meaning of "retention" for contractors.** Another fundamental difference from full-time engagements: when a contractor joins your company it's for a discrete amount of time. Be sure to communicate with your top-performing contractors when they are finishing up their contract. Follow up to see how their engagement was. Express your interest in keeping in touch. Measure—and record—*their* interest and evaluation of their experience at your company.

Preserve Performance Information for the Long Term

Practitioners of TRM understand what it means to select and employ a successful full-time workforce. Contractors work alongside full-time employees—often working for the same managers—

yet the hiring process is kept separate. By getting to know individual contractors' preferences, work styles, and competencies, you'll gain the knowledge of who contributes best to your organization's current success and gain insight into what will bring future success.

Companies should maintain rich profiles on all employees, including contractors. These profiles should grow in complexity over time. When it comes time to make a decision about rehiring, reassigning, or changing the status of a contractor (e.g. from contract to full-time), use all of this information to make the *right* decision.

HR and Procurement Align Themselves at Last

Because contingent talent sourcing tends to be disconnected from FTE hiring, HR and procurement lose the opportunity to create a valuable feedback loop that can generate significant advantages. It's nearly impossible to tell how FTE and contract hiring each contribute to the overall costs to your organization when the processes are not being managed or measured consistently.[6]

As HR consultant Ed Newman writes, "Procurement has very little experience managing and tracking people . . . Companies are spending hundreds of million dollars on contingent labor, but if you ask them to give you a breakdown of their contingent staff—including their skills and the projects they are working on—you would most likely get a blank stare."[7]

By engaging contractors directly and managing the sourcing process on a single TRM platform, HR assumes a much more strategic role in managing an organization's talent. Executives gain complete visibility on full-time and contingent hiring costs, workforce capabilities, and human capital resource allocation. Implementing a direct contractor engagement approach drives direct cost savings in the short term and provides substantial insight for the long term.

Footnotes

1 Ed Newman, "Is Talent Acquisition a Human Resources or Procurement Function?" *ER Daily*, May 14, 2002.

2 American Staffing Association, "Poised for Growth: ASA's Annual Economic Analysis of the Staffing Industry," May/June 2002.

3 This table assumes an average hourly billing rate of $60 for all contractors. The average staffing company mark-up used for cost comparison is 45%.

4 McKinsey & Company, *The War For Talent: New Challenges, New Tactics*, 2001

5 Towers Perrin, *New Realities in Today's Workforce*, 2001

6 Newman, ER Daily, 5/14/2002.

7 Ibid.

CHAPTER TWO

Building Talent Relationships

> "When you do common things in life in an uncommon way, you will, command the attention of the world."

—George Washington Carver

2

In the Trenches: Talent Relationship Management for the Everyday Recruiter

PATRICK LEWSEN

Patrick Lewsen is a senior HR professional, writer, and public speaker. Former Vice President of Business Development at the Newman Group, Vice President of Staffing at Litton PRC, and consultant at AG Consulting, Mr. Lewsen is highly regarded for his consulting work in staffing, workforce planning HRIS, and employee retention. He has authored, developed, implemented, and delivered recruiter training programs throughout the world. Mr. Lewsen can be reached at plewsen@msn.com.

No high-level strategic discussion here, I promise. There seems to be way too much of that lately. I'm talking about in the trenches. About recruiters, tirelessly making phone calls to hundreds of candidates day in and day out and finding ways to be successful in the kind of chaos and uncertainty that a busy recruiter faces each day in trying to live up to the promise of relationship management. Don't get me wrong; the notion of effective long-term relationships with candidates versus point in time casual contact is possible. It can be done with the wise use of a good recruiting technology and some effective organizational skills, but it's no cakewalk.

There should be no doubt that recruiter's face the seemingly impossible task of managing all those relationships. In fact, some of my fondest memories are of dinners out with recruiters who went on all night about the candidate who called back eager to discuss the "opportunity" only to learn that the recruiter had absolutely no idea who they were or why they were calling. Embarrassing at the time but something to relieve stress later. Or the hiring manager who they can't remember or worse whose requisition they completely forgot to work on. Well, I'm sure it doesn't happen to most of you. I've been lucky to meet many recruiters while consulting in this industry and, along with some anecdotes to remember, I've learned some very simple but amazingly effective tricks to help you live up to at least a portion of the ideal of relationship management.

To give those of you who are not recruiters some perspective I'd like to crunch some numbers to try and depict the logistically challenging task of actually managing the relationships a recruiter maintains every day. Let's say Claudia (our recruiter) works in a fortune 100 company, has a rolling thirty-five requisitions, works with ten other recruiters, a recruiting manager, and eighty hiring managers. Claudia's a good recruiter so her hiring ratio is 10:1 (ten contacts for every one hire). Quick, add it up in your head. That makes a whopping 441 "relationships" everyday of the year and it's not the same 441 everyday either. If you consider a hiring cycle of thirty days and throw in a business line shift every two months the relationships grow to a staggering 5000 (I'm estimating a little of coarse). Now wait. It gets better. I forgot all the personal relationships in Claudia's life, but who has time for that.

Now let's make a few assumptions before moving on. Claudia uses one of many recruiting technology systems, has access to the Internet, and has more than one phone line. Also, although it's not a popular idea, lets face the fact that the mercenary recruiter is a transactional machine. Sure, the outcome of that transactional machine is without a doubt the most important part of a company's success and is very strategic indeed. The bigger picture is much more of a human capital strategy discussion than a transactional one but I promised to keep my discussion in the trenches.

So back to Claudia, she's left thirty-five messages yesterday and needs to do more of the same today. Her biggest struggle is dealing with interruptions while trying to make those calls. They usually come in the form of a callback from a candidate so we'll use that example. Dealing with interruptions effectively is the most important thing a good recruiter needs to know to be a good relationship manager. Effectively doing so means always knowing how to get immediately back to where you left off before being interrupted. Claudia does this well by using a key, or something that she always refers to no matter what the interruption. In her case, because she uses a recruiting technology system, it's her requisitions. By always associating *all* her candidate calls with a requisition, Claudia's "my requisitions" is always where she goes when dealing with an interruption.

Claudia has a detailed and specific method of effectively dealing with this type of interruption. First when making calls to potential candidates—90 percent of which result in a voicemail—she makes sure to mention her name several times, the job title several times, and then her contact information followed by another mention of the job title (or reason for calling). Why? Because it's the first step in making sure she can quickly identify the candidate when they call back. Using this technique greatly increases the probability that the candidate's first words are "Hi, this is Patrick, I'm returning your call about the CTO position." Patrick's mention of the CTO job is the information Claudia needs to quickly obtain all the information she needs. Claudia, who most likely still doesn't know who Patrick is, has a starting point and a quick way to find all the information she needs to have a quality, relationship building conversation with Patrick by opening the CTO requisition that she tracked Patrick's record to prior to placing the initial call. She goes to "my requisitions," opens the CTO requisition, and then clicks the button to list all the candidates tracked to the job, one of which is Patrick because Claudia always associates candidates to a requisition before making a call. Even if Claudia isn't recruiting for a "real" requisition, she creates one in the system as a marker or "dummy requisition."

The next part of Claudia's methodology is one of the simplest and cleverest recruiter techniques I've ever seen; it's kind of funny too. You see, Claudia needs time to open the requisition which she's probably not working on at the time of Patrick's call. To find a few seconds to open the requisition without Patrick knowing that she doesn't have the slightest idea of who he is (the infamous paper shuffle), she says "Patrick, I'm so glad you called back, please let me get rid of my other call so we can talk. I'll be right back." Patrick remains on hold and is happy about it, feeling very important to have been the priority for Claudia. Claudia meanwhile opens the CTO requisition, finds his record, and refreshes her memory of the job specifics. When she returns to the call, she knows who he is and can continue with an effective conversation about his qualifications for the CTO job.

Now of course, Claudia could avoid all this if she could only get the person on the phone in the first place. I'm happy to say there are a few tricks for doing that, too. Again they're trench-like and simple but very effective. To get a candidate on the phone most of the time and avoid voicemail follow-up try some of these ideas:

- When voicemail answers, immediately hang-up and call right back. Many candidates who don't answer on the first try will on the second out of curiosity or because they think the call must be important (we've all done it haven't we)

- Call between 7-8:30 AM and 5-7 PM. At these times, people are most commonly at their desks

- Don't be shy about trying all possible numbers; cell phones, pagers, etc. Your call will be important if the person is even remotely a good candidate

Usually the most effective ways to get something done are the simplest. I believe it to be especially true for recruiters. By the way, for those of you who would like to hire Claudia, I'm sorry to say she's a fictional character based on many of the recruiters I've known over the years—you know who you are.

> "Knowledge always desires increases; it is like fire, which must first be kindled by some external agent, but which will afterwards propagate itself."

—Dr. Samuel Johnson

2

The 3 Dimensions of Diversity Recruiting On-line

PETER WEDDLE

Peter Weddle is a recruiter, HR consultant and business CEO turned author and commentator. Described by *The Washington Post* as ". . . a man filled with ingenious ideas," he has earned an international reputation, pioneering such concepts as Human Capital, Career Fitness, and the use of the Internet for recruiting and Human Resource management. Mr. Weddle has authored seven books, edited eleven others and published dozens of articles in professional and trade magazines. He is the publisher of *WEDDLE's,* a monthly newsletter about on-line resources for effective recruiting and retention. Mr. Weddle is a graduate of the United States Military Academy at West Point. He attended Oxford University and holds advanced degrees from Middlebury College and Harvard University. Mr. Weddle can be reached at pdweddle@worldnet.att.net.

Although the "digital divide" remains a nagging problem, the online pool of diversity talent is expanding at an impressive rate. For example, according to an August 2001 Nielsen/NetRatings survey, Internet usage among African-Americans increased by 19 percent over the prior year. That's five percentage points faster than the rate of growth among the overall population and means that there are now almost 8.2 million African-Americans using the Internet. In addition, the time African-Americans spend on-line is also increasing faster (22 percent year-over-year) than among the population at large (12 percent year-over-year).

How can on-line recruiters tap into this trend to enhance their diversity recruiting? I suggest that you implement a three-dimensional on-line strategy that will:

- Place your employment opportunities where your target diversity candidates are most likely to see them on the Internet
- Build your organization's reputation among diversity populations; and
- Create a positive, distinctive experience for the diversity candidates who interact with your organization

Let's take a look at each of these components in more detail.

Advertise at the right sites. While diversity candidates do, in fact, visit all kinds of recruitment sites, from Monster.com to techies.com, they tend to spend considerable time on sites that focus on either their unique affinity (e.g., African-American, Hispanic-American, women) or diversity in general. Hence, recruiters seeking to post jobs and/or search résumé databases for diversity candidates should (a) identify the alternatives among sites that specialize in their target diversity cohort and (b) evaluate those alternatives to determine which are likely to provide their optimum return on investment.

Among the diversity sites listed in *Weddle's 2002 Directory of Employment-Related Internet Sites* (ISBN: 1-928734-06-5) are:

- **Asia-Net** www.asia-net.com
- **Bilingual-Jobs** www.bilingual-jobs.com
- **The Black Collegian Online** www.blackcollegian.com
- **Diversity Careers** www.diversitycareers.com
- **Financial Women International** www.fwi.org
- **iHispano** www.ihispano.com
- **LatPro** www.latpro.com
- **National Black MBA Association** www.nbmbaa.org
- **National Society of Hispanic MBA's** www.nshmba.org
- **Women in Technology International** www.witi.org

As there are now hundreds of such sites in operation on-line, it's important to distinguish between the good and the mediocre. How can you do that? Compare one site to another, using the following factors:

- Traffic, reported in unique visitors per month
- Visitor Attention Span (page views per month/unique visitors per month) which indicates how long visitors stay on a site
- Price per posting or to search the resume database
- Candidate Density (unique visitors per month/jobs posted per month) which measures the competition your posting will face from other postings on the site
- The number of résumés in the site's database and their source
- Top occupations among the resumes archived in the database; and
- Whether or not the site offers a job agent service for job seekers (sites that provide this service tend to attract a higher proportion of passive job seekers as it enables them to protect their confidentiality)

Build your employer's reputation on-line. Posting jobs and searching for résumés at the right sites will help you source top quality diversity candidates, but it will not ensure that you can recruit them. To do that, your organization must build a credible reputation as an organization that is truly committed to providing genuine career opportunities for women, persons of color, and other diversity cohorts.

What steps can you take on-line to establish such a "diversity friendly" brand? Consider the following:

- Ensure that all of the images on your organization's recruitment website—the photos of employees and views of occupied offices—reflect the true diversity of your workforce
- Include an explicit statement about your organization's commitment to diversity on the site's home page

Don't overlook age discrimination. Make sure that you post all of your open positions on your website, including those in which more senior (and often older) job seekers might be interested.

- Add a similar statement about your organization's diversity commitment to every job posting on your site and include the statement in the auto-responder message you send back to all applicants
- If you are posting individual "success stories" touting the kind of employee who works for you (and I urge you to do so), make sure that those who are selected reflect the diversity of your workforce
- Don't overlook age discrimination. Make sure that you post *all* of your open positions on your website, including those in which more senior (and often older) job seekers might be interested
- Sponsor key features and events on commercial diversity websites and, if possible, on the alumni sites of colleges and universities that have historically served specific ethnic groups, women, and those with physical disabilities
- Also have recruiters (and/or selected employees) participate in newsgroups, listservs, and discussion boards that focus on topics of particular interest to diversity candidates (e.g., soc.culture.african.american, soc.culture.cuba)

Provide a distinctive candidate experience. Sourcing at the right sites and presenting an attractive value proposition will attract a larger and deeper pool of diversity prospects to your organization, but it will not necessarily get the best candidate to accept your offer. The key to successfully converting top quality prospects into new hires is an extraordinary candidate experience. In other words, what happens to each individual during the recruitment process must make real and reinforce the organization's commitment to equal employment opportunity. It must give them a taste of the organization that is believable and proves it walks the talk, that diversity is not just the EEO/AA acronym on job ads, but a true value of the organization.

The key to successfully converting top quality prospects into new hires is an extraordinary candidate experience.

Earning such credibility takes time, perseverance, and visible initiatives. These actions include:

- Training recruiters and hiring managers to be bias free in their interviews and other interactions with candidates, to include the terms and phrases they use in their e-mail communications

- Establishing a special area on the organization's website devoted to diversity candidates and highlighting there both the commitment to diversity of the organization's senior leaders and the information that diversity candidates want to make informed employment decisions

- Providing access, via the website, to current employees from various diversity cohorts so that candidates in those same cohorts can get private, candid feedback on what it's like to work in the organization

- Assigning to each diversity candidate a "process mentor" who shares their background and is available via e-mail to answer questions and address concerns as the recruitment process unfolds.

Thanks to growing Internet usage across all segments of the American population, on-line recruiting is no longer limited to a "World White Web." In order to take full advantage of this shift, however, recruiters must be proactive about the sites they use for job postings and résumé acquisition, the image they create on-line for their organization and the experience they provide to each diversity candidate during the recruitment process. Get those three-dimensions right, and you'll give your organization a powerful competitive advantage in the search for top diversity talent.

> "To accept good advice is but to increase one's own ability."

—Johann Wolfgang von Goethe

2

The Human Element of Recruiting

KEN GAFFEY

Ken Gaffey is an independent human resources and staffing consultant with an extensive and in-depth career of diversified human resources and staffing experience in the high-tech, financial services, manufacturing, and pharmaceutical industries. In addition to contributing articles and book reviews to publications like ERE, Monster.com, AIRS, *HR Today*, and the *International Recruiters Newsletter*, Mr. Gaffey is a frequent speaker at international conferences, training seminars, and other staffing industry events. He is an active member of IHRCA, NEHRA, SHRM, HRC, EMA, the Society of Professional Consultants, and the Human Resources Council. Mr. Gaffey can be reached at kengaffey@earthlink.net.

Receptionist: XYZ Corporation, can I help direct your call?

Caller: Yes, I'd like to speak to someone in staffing/recruitment please.

Receptionist: Certainly. I'll connect you to our IT department.

Caller: No, no, I didn't say I wanted to work in IT. I said I wanted to speak to someone in recruiting!

Receptionist: There is no one specifically in recruiting anymore. IT is now responsible for most of the recruiting functions.

Caller: IT does your recruiting? What, aren't you guys hiring?"

Receptionist: Of course we are; we have several critical needs. But between the on-line résumé banks, automated search engines, search agents, automated prescreening, on-line testing, automated routing, on-line requisitions and position descriptions, interactive scheduling software, and e-mail management tools, it seemed the people in staffing and recruiting were so busy managing the tools they never got around to being hands-on recruiters involved in the actual recruiting process itself.

Caller: Recruiters not recruiting? How could that happen?

Receptionist: Well, they thought they were recruiting. It's just that somehow they assumed that the people-end of recruiting was secondary. As a matter of fact, many of our recruiters were our worst people-persons. They were hired almost exclusively for their perceived skills as e-recruiters, not recruiters. The managers took on more and more of the person-to-person aspect of staffing, and soon the system appeared to be pumping résumés into the bin without any direct involvement of the staffing group. Then one day, after a staff meeting, the CEO said that based on the levels and topics of discussions, he could no longer tell the difference between his VP of staffing and his chief information officer. He figured he didn't need to pay for two IT departments, so we combined them. As a matter of fact, one of the people who used to be a senior technical recruiter just upgraded my PC and fixed my printer. He seemed happy in IT. Got himself a little tool belt and everything.

Caller: Really? Well, didn't staffing and recruiting say anything at the time about their professional contribution to the process beyond the technology?

Receptionist: I think they were so busy looking into an on-line tool that would eliminate the need for human-to-human interaction in the interview process that they didn't notice what was going on 'til the lights went out.

Caller: So now all your recruiting is handled by IT?

Receptionist: Most of it, except for recruiting communications, which is done by our webmaster. He already was doing marketing/communications anyway, but he always seems to be selling product, not opportunity. Negotiations are done by our finance group—if you call mailing an offer without discussions negotiations. They developed a price list like the one they did for purchasing. The concept sounded good.

Caller: What about HR?

Receptionist: Gone. We outsourced so much of their work before all this happened that the only job they had left was managing staffing, and when that went to IT . . ."

Caller: I see what you are saying. So how is it working out?

Receptionist: Well, just between you and me, it isn't. We have so many third parties involved in staffing now that our cost per hire is through the roof. The quality isn't there either, and time to fill is measured in decades.

Caller: Well, isn't that cause for alarm!

Receptionist: Nah! Everybody has reports, charts, graphs, and spreadsheets that prove they are actually processing six times the number of résumés that used to be process by the old pre-Internet recruiting team. Somewhere along the line I guess processing résumés and recruiting got confused with each other. You know the old saying, "If it doesn't make sense, just do a PowerPoint presentation and use lots of colors, graphs, and pie charts salted with and new age words, and everybody will forget the purpose in favor of the outcome."

Caller: So despite all the automation, you still are not hiring as many people by your own efforts as you used to?

Receptionist: Well, in my opinion we have all sorts of people *doing* staffing, but nobody who is staffing, do you know what I mean? Ironically, in the end, neither was staffing. They were trying so hard to be e-recruiters that they became too much "e" and not enough "recruiter." The profession attracted people who wanted to manage an on-line processes and load upgrades. A generation of staffing that resisted the part of the process that required working with the people, internal and external. The people who needed to project themselves the most became as introverted as firmware engineers. If it wasn't software driven, they had no time for it. I guess that's why so many of them are doing so well in IT! Turns out a lot of them were closet Star Trek fans anyway.

Caller: You certainly are knowledgeable about staffing and corporate history for a receptionist.

Receptionist: Oh, I was the director of staffing here, but there weren't enough openings in IT for everyone. But, how can I help you?

Caller: Well, I'm looking for a sales job. You still have a sales department, right?

Receptionist: Are you crazy! Of course we do, we would never get rid of sales. Next to hiring top quality people, sales is the most important function in any company . . . Oh, I see what you are getting at. No, we did not totally lose our minds. But sales never forgot who they were or what was important. We were never allowed the chance to confuse their personal contribution with the tools they used. So, can I connect you to someone about employment?

Caller: Ah, no. Thank you anyway. I think you people are too sophisticated for me. You see, I still like working with people and using tools, not working with tools and using people!

Am I talking down automation and electronic recruiting? Heck of a thing for someone who writes for ERE to do!

Of course not! But today I feel the need to stress that which I usually only elude to.

Recruiting is a profession that consists of as much art—if not more—as it does science. A good recruiter embraces the science. But a great recruiter embraces it without becoming ensnared in one tool or another. The tool remains as such and all tools are regarded as merely one of many.

That is to say, the Internet does not recruit.

In essence, the Web is an electronic filing cabinet with storage, search, and communications capability (it also has neat graphics and can play music). It supports, but it does not recruit—just as newspapers did not recruit, nor job fairs, nor open houses, nor radio spots, nor any other venues. They communicated an idea to leads and informed prospects, but they did not recruit.

Fifteen years ago, when the fax first became a fixture in staffing departments and recruiting offices, we did not call ourselves "fax recruiters." We did not elevate the tool to an art. We thought more of ourselves than that; we placed a higher value to our personal contribution than that.

You do not recruit on-line. You can:

- Source
- Advertise
- Generate leads
- Screen prospects
- Inform, advise, be informed, and be advised of all things objective

- Test and analyze to a point of plausibility, but not certainty
- Select for further processing or select to discontinue

But you do not recruit. This may appear to be an issue of semantics, but if you misuse a word often enough, other people assume it must be true. If you talk about recruiting as if it is occurring within your corporate server with no human input, don't be surprised if your role is determined to be more of a technician than an artist.

Recruiting begins when you take all the information and knowledge gained from your tools and you actually contact a candidate:

- With a defined goal other than continued non-committal information exchange
- With the intent to clarify that which can only be clarified by human contact
- With the intent to verify and expand on information only assumed to be correct to this point
- With the intent to focus on one possibility or explore the potential for more
- With the intent to pursue and not merely process
- With the goal to terminate if that is the best course of action
- With the intent to control

A sales professional does not confuse the advertising and pre-sales research he or she does, or the tools they use to conduct that advertising and research, with the actual art of "selling." Sales professionals recognize that in each deal a part of their process is using specialized automation tools to assist them in the more productive use of their time, decreasing the number of cycles they have to spend in the "non-sales" part of selling process. They are equally aware that the average 16-year-old could also be trained to use these same tools if the only goal of the process was amassing data.

The art of selling is using that data to bring about a result that neither the tool nor the 16-year-old can accomplish without help. This is the element of the process that separates the skilled practitioner from the technologist: their involvement using the interpersonal and project management skills they have honed over the years in their career.

Once upon a time the only people you could be directly connected with in any company were sales and staffing. Both departments realized that all policies, procedures, tools, budget items, training, and daily work effort were nothing more than an attempt to get prospects to make human-to-human contact. That is when the "artist" goes to work; the technicians' work is finished. But today, most staffing groups shield themselves from incoming calls by either not giving their phone number or "hiding" behind their voicemail. Might as well be calling HR (ouch!).

The human skills you develop are a constant in your career. Little has changed in the basics of human interaction in the last over fifty years, nor will it in the next fifty to come. But the mechanical and technical tools we use change at least twice a decade. Right now someone is probably working on a nano-liquified-helium-based communication device that will revolutionize technology and replace the Internet. Anybody want to be called a "Helium Recruiter"?

As automation absorbs the recruiting process, most companies see the opportunity to reduce staff—the age-old purpose of automation. But the company that truly understands recruiting knows that quality recruiting is not only labor intensive, but more importantly, human-labor intensive. Automation is not the tool to cut cost, but the tool to free a fixed base of recruiters to invest more cycles in the real art of recruiting: dealing with the people in the process.

But the company that truly understands recruiting knows that quality recruiting is not only labor intensive, but more importantly, human-labor intensive.

You can supplement your recruitment tool portfolio with a checkbook, but the human skills come much harder, contribute more to the process and are not easily replaced. Do not let those you support assume your contribution to the process can be found on a CD. More importantly, do not assume that yourself. Until you are satisfied with the quality of hiring—the eternal pursuit of the top 10 percent—you have too few recruiters working on too many requisitions, despite your level of automation. The automation serves the data-processing portion, the recruiters recruit. Hence the name. If your company thinks that recruiting is merely another bothersome task to be automated into oblivion, who do you think taught them to think that way?

Who speaks for the recruiters in your staffing process? More importantly, who will be answering your phones this time next year?

Have a great day recruiting!

> "You can dream, create, design, and build the most wonderful place in the world. . . . but it requires *people* to make the dream a reality."

—Walt Disney

2

The Value of Relationships in Your Talent Inventory

CARY SMITH

Cary Smith is a talent officer based in Austin, TX. His independent thinking has fueled new ideas in the areas of recruiting culture, staffing systems, talent supply management, and employment branding. Smith's comprehensive experience includes eight years in corporate staffing and recruiting systems. He played a lead role in the formation of Motorola's first candidate sourcing effort, and was formerly the talent officer at Hire.com. He currently works with Fortune 500 companies to create dynamic employment brands, install recruiting cultures, implement staffing systems, and promote talent supply management practices. Mr. Smith can be reached at cary@thetalentofficer.com.

Last week, I watched my local grocer unload produce from a truck, and it got me thinking. I asked the store manager how fast he had to sell his inventory before it spoiled. Typically, he told me, a head of lettuce will last about two weeks from the time it hits the grocery dock. After two weeks, the produce spoils and must be discarded. Since the store takes a loss on spoiled produce, the grocer recognizes that he needs to sell his lettuce in a timely manner if he's going to run a profitable operation.

Aside from being completely boring, the unloading of produce reminds me of the recruiting process that most companies have in place today. To me, résumés are just like lettuce. The staffing organization spends time and money to generate résumés and then stores them in a résumé warehouse. From there the recruiting team attempts to match candidates to jobs, and any lost, unused, non-matching, or unwanted résumés just sit. After a short time, the unused résumés "go bad," and eventually your résumé warehouse has completely spoiled. In this scenario, there is no future value to generating a vast résumé database. All you can do is continue to spend additional resources to generate more résumé "lettuce" to replace the stock that spoils from year to year.

But talent officers, if they are interested in improving the recruiting function, should create a process that allows for a return on the candidates that are not immediately unused but could be useful in the future. To do this, the staffing organization should recruit for relationships.

Relationships are not like lettuce, because they are durable and can last indefinitely. A staffing process that is relationship-based drives value into the talent inventory because the relationship remains intact over time. Relationship recruiting also impacts the staffing operation in two powerful ways: it reduces the cost to acquire new talent and it reduces overall recruiting volume.

Reducing the Cost to Acquire New Talent

In a lettuce-based recruiting process, the staffing organization pays maximum costs because it generates a talent inventory that is not durable. Over time, you will lose a certain percentage of unused relationships and increase the number of new relationships you must generate in the future. Using the lettuce-based recruiting process also has a theoretical cost associated with lost or spoiled talent inventory.

Last year, a major computer manufacturer I know of used the lettuce process. This organization spent $150 million, hired 26,000 people, and generated 700,000 résumés. Although they hired many people as a result, there was no return on investment for the unused résumés they generated. If you do the math, you can quickly see that each résumé cost them about $215. Since the balance of résumés were not used, and subsequently spoiled, you can then calculate a talent inventory loss of $144 million.

Next year, they will probably spend about the same amount of money, hire about the same amount of people, and incur the same loss. Ouch . . . don't let the CFO see this!

But if we consider a relationship-based recruiting process, we see that the talent inventory is durable and will not spoil rapidly over time. Because the relationships are nurtured and sustained, a company can retain an inventory that does not need replacement nearly as often as the lettuce-based recruiting process's does. This inventory retention effect requires less and less recruiting resources each year, as the durable talent inventory grows and meets more of the requirements of future staffing plans.

Suppose, for example, that in 2001 we spend $100 million and generate 100,000 relationships (a cost of $1,000 per relationship). Out of those 100,000 relationships we hire 25,000 people. Let's assume the remaining 75,000 relationships will endure and possibly become viable candidates for next year. In 2001, unused talent inventory has an associated inventory cost of $75 million (75,000 relationships x $1,000 per relationship). We can expect that some relationships will leave the talent inventory, but for the purposes of illustration we will assume that no relationships are lost over the course of the year.

In 2002, we have 75,000 previously established relationships. To accomplish 2002 hiring goals, we need to get our talent inventory back to 100,000 relationships. But we need only recruit 25,000

In relationship recruiting you can develop a recruiting horizon that maximizes productivity and minimizes cost.

new relationships, because we already have 75,000 retained relationships in our talent inventory. Using this math, the staffing organization can then expect to spend only $25 million toward new relationship acquisitions for this year, based on our $1000-per-relationship calculation. Theoretically, the result is a $75 million dollar savings over 2001 staffing expenditures in 2002.

Now, keep in mind that there will always be some attrition from the relationship database as people obtain jobs or change career interests. For illustration purposes, assume that relationships are lost unless they are hired by the organization. In reality, there will be many factors that cause a relationship to terminate, and the talent officer would need to account for these factors when developing a staffing plan.

Reducing the Volume of New Talent Needs

If you are using a lettuce-based recruiting process, you will always be in a résumé-generating mode. Each year requires that you generate more résumés, with no foreseeable end in sight. In most cases, staffing organizations also purge any unused or spoiled résumés to make room for newly generated résumés.

In relationship recruiting you can develop a recruiting horizon that maximizes productivity and minimizes cost. This horizon is a theoretical point in the future where you have all relationships you need to fill all positions. The staffing team draws only from the established relationship base and recruits only for lost or hired relationships. The talent officer can even use a relationship recruiting process to project the date of the recruiting horizon and develop a plan accordingly.

To illustrate this point, assume that from 2001 to 2003 you will have to fill 1,000 jobs per year. From past experience you know that it takes roughly ten candidates to fill one position. That means that you will have to recruit 10,000 applicants in 2001 to satisfy your staffing needs. In 2001, you hire 1,000 people and the relationship base is now at 9,000. In 2002, you have to fill another 1,000 positions, but already have 9,000 viable relationships to draw from. This means that you only need to attract another 1,000 relationships to satisfy your 2002 staffing plan, provided that the 9,000 established relationships do not fill your needs.

In 2003, the situation is the same as in 2002, where you are operating at the recruiting horizon. You are only recruiting for relationships that you hired or lost from the relationship base. Because it minimizes the overall number of new relationships needed to fill the staffing plan, the recruiting horizon is the most productive and cost effective state for the staffing team. It may take many years to attain the recruiting horizon, as some companies have thousands of openings that require hundreds of thousands of applicants to satisfy the need. But I estimate that when the recruiting horizon is reached, the staffing organization will be spending about 10 percent to 20 percent of their current run rate.

To fundamentally impact the basic recruiting process requires a paradigm shift in the staffing organization's thinking. Recruiting for relationships is only one piece in a new recruiting paradigm, but it is one that will result in less volume and higher return on previous staffing efforts. Talent officers looking to improve their recruiting functions will strive to eliminate the lettuce-based recruiting process and to develop a process that creates more and more value for their companies as each year passes.

CHAPTER THREE

Nurturing Talent to Succeed and Stay

> "The greater the difficulty, the more glory in surmounting it."

—Epicurus

3

Winning the Talent War with a TRM Hiring Strategy

LOU ADLER

Lou Adler is a veteran recruiter and founder of CJA Executive Search, a national firm headquartered in Southern California. He's also the creator and CEO of POWER Hiring—Best Practices for Hiring Top People. Lou is author of *Hire With Your Head, A Rational Way to Make a Gut Decision* (John Wiley and Sons, 1998), and the award-winning Nightingale Conant audio tape program, *POWER Hiring: How to Find, Assess, Hire and Keep Great Talent* (1999). His new book, *25 Things You Must Do to Hire Great People Every Time*, will be published in late 2002. He holds an MBA from UCLA and a BS in Engineering from Clarkson University, New York. Mr. Adler can be reached at lou@powerhiring.com.

Every manager says that hiring great people is their most important task, however, few walk the talk. Although important, it never seems urgent enough until it's too late. If you're a manager, right now rank the performance of every member of your own team. Are most of them top-notch and exceeding expectations? If they are, consider yourself a strong manager. If you're a recruiter, ask your clients how good the candidates you recommended to be hired actually are performing. Are they all in the top-third, or better yet, the top 10 percent? Unless you're hiring or recommending the best 80 to 90 percent of the time, you need to reconsider everything you've learned or know about hiring, and start with a fresh new Talent Relationship Management (TRM) perspective.

Hiring Is Too Important to Leave to Chance

If you want to hire superior people, use a process and system designed to hire superior people, not one designed to fill jobs. The emphasis of too many hiring processes is to reduce costs and fill jobs as rapidly as possible. Instead, hiring the best must dominate every aspect of a company's hiring process. This is the clear theme of the latest McKinsey Consulting research project, *The*

War for Talent.[1] The authors surveyed over 200 major companies. The conclusions were obvious—hiring the best is an essential component of long term success requiring a comprehensive and well-executed plan. Talk is not enough.

In the mid-90s everyone thought the Internet was going to be the new tool that allowed everyone to hire great people quickly and at low cost. It wasn't. For 2001, surveys indicate that less than 10 percent of all hires came from job boards.[2] And this was the best year ever! Trends indicate that the use of job boards won't grow by much more. There's much more to hiring great people than posting an ad.

If you want to hire superior people, use a process and system designed to hire superior people, not one designed to fill jobs.

Hiring the best requires a TRM system and process designed around the needs of hiring the best people. Part of the reason a formal hiring system and process is so important is that the people involved in the hiring process are often untrained and unsophisticated when it comes to hiring. Most of the biggest causes of hiring mistakes are due to the people involved in the hiring process: candidates, recruiters, hiring managers and interviewers. Few are trained, few standards are imposed, and few metrics exist. In reality, we don't plan to hire the best, we hope for it. Here are some examples of what happens when we focus on filling jobs, not hiring the best:

- We develop systems that make it too hard for the best candidates to apply for job openings. We impose hurdles that only desperate candidates will jump. The best opt-out instead. For example, the best will relocate for the right opportunity, but they'll never consider it on the first phone call or as part of a questionnaire. Most application processing systems are designed with the active job seeker in mind. As the supply of active top candidates tightens, different on-line approaches need to be used.

- Recruiters and hiring managers are looking for different candidates (the moving job description). Managers complain that recruiters don't really know how to assess candidate competency, and recruiters complain that managers won't spend the time necessary to do it right. Unless recruiters and hiring managers are on the same page, this classic bottleneck will strangle any chance of consistently hiring top people.
- Emotions, biases, prejudices, and first impressions dominate the hiring decision. When we like a candidate we minimize problems, and start selling. When we don't like a candidate, we look for a few good reasons to exclude them. Then we wonder why the candidates hired aren't as good as we thought. Unfortunately, the best were let go for all the wrong reasons.
- We ignore how the best make hiring decisions. For one, the best take longer to decide and they want more information. For them a new job is the beginning of a career. For the rest, a new job is the end of an ordeal. The best want the interview to be challenging, not easy. A job has more value this way. How many great people did you let slip away by moving too fast, overselling, or through just plain unprofessional or superficial behavior? Few companies have thought through how the needs of top candidates are implemented into their systems.

Plan on hiring the best, don't hope for it. You'll be disappointed.

It Starts with Looking at Sourcing from a TRM Perspective

The best candidates want careers, not jobs. Unfortunately most companies are just offering jobs. For immediate proof, look at ten random ads on any job board. Each describes a job in terms of skills, experience, and requirements. They don't describe career challenges or opportunities for growth. If you want to attract the best people, you need to attract them with the best jobs. Make each page on your career site a marketing piece. Make each job description exciting. Treat candidates as customers.

Top candidates don't evaluate jobs the same way average candidates do. For the best, accepting the job is a long-term strategic decision.

Even a top candidate who is looking for a job has multiple opportunities. In a slow economy there are more top people looking, but you still need to offer something more than just another job if you want to attract their interest. In normal economic times you'll want to attract top candidates who are not actively looking. They'll be willing to explore a better opportunity, but they won't even consider just another job. Companies lose out on hiring the best by not understanding that the best want careers, not jobs. If you're not an employer-of-choice with top candidates knocking down your door, you'd better offer a great job. This is the performance profile, the P in POWER. It describes a job in terms of challenges, major accomplishments, and team building needs. Describing a great job is the first step in finding great candidates.

Top candidates don't evaluate jobs the same way average candidates do. For the best, accepting the job is a long-term strategic decision. It involves outside advisors including friends and family. They take longer to decide and want more information. Recruiting these top candidates needs to be a career management counseling process, not a transaction. This is the R in POWER, Recruiting Right. You can't oversell these candidates. You'll either lose them, or wind up paying an unnecessary premium. Instead you must demonstrate how your open opportunity compares favorably to all other jobs under consideration. It's like trying to sell a custom product through the Yellow Pages. It can't be done. Yet few recruiters are trained to be career counselors. If they're not, you'll lose top candidates every step of the way.

Why You Should Throw Away Everything You Know about Hiring

The common interview, the one used by most managers, is a flawed means to hire anyone. Emotions, biases, chemistry, and stereotypes play too big a role. The competency of the interviewer is questionable. True knowledge of the job is weak. Some candidates give misleading information because they're not asked appropriate questions. Others are nervous. Standards fall as desperation grows. Some of these problems can be eliminated just by knowing their causes.

One of the biggest problems is that too much emphasis is placed on the interaction between the candidate and the interviewer, and too little on the candidate's ability and motivation to do the job. This is the number one cause of hiring mistakes. Over the past twenty-five years I've been personally involved in over 1,000 different interviewing situations. From this it's clear that most of the hiring decision is influenced by the interpersonal relationship developed early in the interview between the applicant and the hiring manager. Sometimes this can be in as little as a few minutes. This has to do with chemistry, first impressions, emotions, biases, stereotypes, the halo effect (globalizing a few strengths), and the tendency to hire in one's image.

In most cases real job needs are poorly understood, and even if they are well understood, they're filtered through these interpersonal relationships and biases. This is how randomness enters the hiring process. If you like a candidate you tend to go into chat mode, ask easier questions, and look for information to confirm you initial impression. If you don't like someone, you put up a defense shield, ask tougher questions, and try to end the interview quickly. You go out of your way to find information to prove your initial impression that the candidate is incompetent.

In both cases the hiring assessment is inaccurate because the wrong things are being assessed. The candidate's ability to get the job is what's really being measured, not the candidate's ability to do the job. Presentation is more important than substance. Moving the decision making process from "getting" to "doing" is hard work and mentally challenging. It's especially difficult when we need to counteract the natural tendency to judge people based on first impression, personality, and a few select traits. If you can overcome this problem, you'll quickly eliminate 50 percent of all common hiring errors. The lack of real job knowledge represents much of the balance. The majority of hiring errors can be eliminated when both issues are addressed together.

Five Steps to Getting Hiring Right—An Introduction to TRM-Focused Hiring

Any one of the problems noted above can cause the hiring process to collapse. Over the past twenty-five years, I've been studying the hiring process in an attempt to figure out what works best. What was very interesting was what those companies and managers who consistently hired top people did just about everything differently from those who hired average people. More surprising, the people who hired the best did everything pretty much the same way. The common methods these best managers used to hire the best candidates eventually became the five basic POWER Hiring principles described below. When combined with an automated hiring management system, these principles help illustrate the art and science of TRM. Try them out for yourself. Once you do you'll start hiring some great people.

The Five POWER Hiring Principles for Hiring Great People

Performance Profiles
. . . if you want to hire superior people, first define superior performance

Objective Evaluations
. . . past performance is a best predictor of future performance

Well-developed Sourcing Plans
. . . sourcing is marketing, not advertising

Emotional Control
. . . measure personality and performance, but measure performance first

Recruiting Right
. . . recruiting is career counseling, not selling. Candidates then sell you

The "**P**" in POWER stands for **Performance Profiles**. This is the most important of all of the principles, since it impacts all of the others. If you want to hire superior people you first must define superior performance. Traditional job descriptions define skills. Define success instead. Define what the best do with the skills. Focus on what the person must do, not what the person must have. This will go a long way toward improving your hiring decisions. Then get everyone on the interviewing team to agree. Once superior performance is defined and agreed upon, it's much easier to find superior people. If you don't clearly define superior performance, everyone will substitute their own perceptions and stereotypes. This is how the hiring process begins to fall apart.

The "**O**" in POWER stands for **Objective Evaluation**. Once performance expectations are defined, all interviewers must use an objective, performance-based approach to determine if the candidate is both competent and motivated to do the work. Start by obtaining detailed examples of a candidate's five or six major accomplishments. Spend ten to fifteen minutes on each one to understand the process used to achieve the accomplishment and the environment in which it took place. This is where you need to train candidates to give you all the information you need. Then examine these accomplishments over time to develop trends and compare these to real job needs. Combine this with reference checks, testing, panel interviews, and take-home tests. Collectively, this will get you into the 80 percent plus accuracy range.

The "**W**" in POWER stands for **Wide-Ranging Sourcing**. The quality of the hiring decision first depends on the quality of the sourcing program. A good proactive multi-tiered sourcing program is a critical component of an effective hiring program. It must include compelling advertising that offers careers, not just jobs, and a strong employee referral program. Sourcing also must be proactive. For most companies, hiring is needs driven. If you only start looking when you need someone, you've just lost the advantage of time. Desperation is the second most significant cause of hiring mistakes. Fill the pipeline and start sourcing at least 90-120 days before you need the candidate.

The "**E**" in POWER represents **Emotional Control**. While desperation is the second basic cause of hiring mistakes, it directly impacts the primary cause of hiring errors—the lack of emotional control. More hiring mistakes are made based on emotional reactions and gut feelings than any other single reason. The emotional link between the interviewer and the candidate must be broken in order to remain objective. We're programmed to make major decisions based on first impressions. If positive, we tend to be less discriminating. If negative, we hold the applicant to a higher standard, or ignore their responses entirely. It's important to measure both performance and personality, but measure personality through the candidate's accomplishment, not by how friendly or attractive the person is.

The "**R**" in POWER stands for **Recruiting Right**. Eventually you'll meet a candidate you want to hire. Good recruiting skills then become essential. Recruiting is the process of persuading a candidate to take the job and then closing all of the details. Most managers believe recruiting is the ability to sell or charm a candidate about the merits and terms of the position. This is the least effective form of recruiting. Emotional control is a critical need at this point. Once we meet a great candidate their is a tendency to start selling. If you oversell you cheapen the job. That's why good recruiting is more counseling than selling. By creating a compelling career opportunity the candidate is more likely to sell you, rather than the other way around. Recruiting is an essential aspect of a well-developed hiring program. It's the final piece toward building a great team.

Key TRM Steps to Effective Hiring

Hiring the best needs to be designed into every system. Here's the short list of what's needed to get hiring right:

1. Target the best. Create careers, not jobs. Hiring the best is a solution, not a transaction.

2. Be proactive. Hiring requires forward-looking planning. This gives you the time to use all available sourcing options.

3. Clearly understand the performance needs of the job. Define success, not skills, and then get everyone to agree.

4. Control the impact of first impressions. Emotional biases are the number one source of hiring errors. Measure performance, before personality. In fact, measure first impressions at the end of the interview when you're not affected by it. You'll see the difference immediately.

5. Measure job competency, not interviewing skills. Train candidates to give complete comprehensive information about accomplishments. Don't accept generalities. Do this for all candidates, whether you like them or not. You'll discover a third of the candidates you thought were great, are really pretty average. And about a third of those you initially thought were weak, will turn out to be much better.

This requires new sourcing and advertising programs, new ways of thinking, changes in writing job descriptions, emotional control, and different interviewing and recruiting techniques. Good hiring is a system not an event. In order to consistently find and hire top people, the hiring process must become a core business process planned and designed around a company's strategic initiatives. Hiring the best is too important to leave to chance.

Endnotes

1 Michaels, Handfield-Jones, Axelrod. *The War for Talent.* Harvard Business School Press. 2001.

2 Jerry Crispin and Mark Mehler, *CareerXRoads.* 2001.

> "Our moral responsibility is not to stop the future but to shape it . . . to channel our destiny in humane directions and to ease the trauma of transition."

—Futurist, Alvin Toffler

3

Antidote to High Turnover: Talent Relationship Management

GREGORY P. SMITH

Gregory P. Smith is the Founder and President of Chart Your Course International, a Georgia-based management consulting firm focusing on building high performance organizations. A leading authority on employee talent management, retention, and leadership, Mr. Smith has been featured in *Business Week*, *Kiplinger's Personal Finance*, *President,* and *CEO*. He has conducted management training programs worldwide and to many well-known companies including Yamaha, Delta Airlines, Turner Broadcasting, Wyndham Hotels, UNISYS, and Hallmark Cards. Listed in Harvard University's *Profile in Business and Management: An International Directory of Scholars and Their Research*, his websites are www.ChartCourse.com and www.HighRetention.com. Mr. Smith can be reached at Greg@chartcourse.com.

The antidote to high turnover is *talent relationship management* (TRM)—the process of attracting, selecting, caring, training, developing, and keeping a workforce to perform their jobs in an organization.

Talent relationship management has as its ultimate goal creating a work environment that allows good employees to stay as long as possible . . . allows mismatched employees to leave sooner or find more compatible jobs elsewhere . . . and allows employees to become more productive.

Although some employees may be more vulnerable than others—a good IT engineer may get three to four job offers each week—every employee contributes to the bottom line. Even a customer service person in a laundromat or a server in a restaurant is a key employee, especially if he/she makes each customer's experience as pleasant and productive as possible. His/her departure would definitely impact corporate customers and the success of the business. So, while you might want to invest many more dollars in strategies for high-priced, high-profile, hard-to-replace executives, it is important to spend time and money on everyone. In a tight job market, recruiters and other employers feel no shame

Accept the fact that 30 to 50 percent of your workforce is considering leaving your job for another.

about shopping for good people inside your organization. If someone offers a service that another company wants, he or she is vulnerable.

No matter what kind of job your people work in, someone is looking to steal them away. Don't blindly believe that your employees are happy and content. Just because you are happy and content in your job doesn't mean everyone who works for you is. Accept the fact that 30 to 50 percent of your workforce is considering leaving your job for another. They may be perfectly happy with their job and still think about leaving. Thirty percent of the respondents to my survey answered "yes" to the question, "Are you presently considering leaving your job for another?" Another six percent answered "maybe."

A Great Return on Investment

The first and foremost reason to practice TRM is cost. Even a small effort can save plenty of money. Studies show that at minimum, it costs $4,000-$7,000 to replace an hourly low-wage employee and up to $40,000 to replace a mid-level, salaried employee. One Silicon Valley company I know estimates that the cost of replacing the average employee is $125,000. The Saratoga Institute and Hewitt Associates estimate that the productivity cost of replacing employees can cost between 1 to 2.5 times of the salary of the job opening. The annual impact of multiple departures can be staggering.

The most effective strategy is prevention. Recruiting and replacing your workforce is much more expensive. Spending most of your time on recruiting is like having your house burn down instead of purchasing a smoke detector—or having your lung removed instead of quitting smoking. Prevention is always less expensive, and wiser, especially when it comes to replacing top performers.

Consider the economic cost of replacing these key individuals:

- Average engineer in Silicon Valley—$200K
- Engineer at Cisco—$250K
- Top microchip product development team leader—$29 million
- Airline Pilot who makes a mistake—??

Why Doesn't Everyone Use Talent Relationship Management?

In spite of the staggering cost of turnover, Development Dimensions International says that 54 percent of businesses do not have a formal retention program. On my survey, 61 percent of the respondents gave their organizations a failing grade on the question, *"How would you rate the efforts of your company to retain good people?"*

Why don't these organizations have retention programs?

- Blind acceptance that certain jobs have high turnover
- Failure to accept responsibility for retaining good people
- Responsibility for retention seen as HR's alone—not management's
- Belief that a counteroffer can prevent losing a good employee
- Unaware how much turnover really costs the bottom line
- Feel it takes too much time
- No management accountability system.

Reasons to have a TRM program:

- Improve company reputation
- Reduce turnover of critical employees
- Keep competitors from stealing your workers
- Positive word-of-mouth from existing employees
- Increase productivity
- Reduce costs and time spent replacing workers
- Simplify time and effort for managers
- Knowledge stays with the company
- Good companies attracts good people
- Remove the stigma of returning to your organization if other job doesn't work out.

Talent Relationship Management Process

To find out whether you need a TRM process, write "yes" or "no" on a separate sheet of paper for each statement.

1. I measure the jobs in my organization that have the highest turnover.
2. I conduct post-exit interviews thirty to ninety days after the employee leaves the organization to find out the real reason he left.
3. I hold my managers accountable for turnover in their department.
4. I reward my managers for high retention in their department.
5. A part of every meeting is dedicated to staff retention and morale.

6. We have a good orientation program for new employees.
7. We go out of our way to communicate with our employees.

If you get more than two "no's" you need to get serious about TRM.

Retention Means Productivity

Costs alone won't persuade you to invest in a retention strategy. Consider the issue of productivity.

Productivity and retention go hand in hand. Improve one, and you improve the other. Why?

Many traditional, hierarchical-based organizations restrict the free exchange of ideas and discourage individual initiative and motivation. After all, ideas and initiative create change—and many systems simply don't want to. They protect themselves with complex bureaucracy and unwieldy procedures that become obstacles to productivity. Workers become slaves of the system. They end up feeling blocked, unchallenged, and little more than robots waiting for the next command.

Constant reorganizations, a stultifying routine, co-workers with bad attitudes, micromanagement, suspicious management, no authority to fix errors or implement ideas, people who play the "who can stay latest" game—all these are impediments to productivity as well as an incentive to leave. No one really wants to work—or can—in this kind of environment!

Retention means nothing if workers merely take up space. In a survey conducted by the Public Agenda Foundation in New York, 50 percent of the respondents said they fail to put effort into their job over and beyond what is required. Three out of four people said they had the capability of becoming more effective than they were.

In a high-retention work environment, employees *can* become more effective. If you pay people well and provide good leadership—create a sense of belonging and purpose and eliminate the frustration of constant reorganization that drives people out the door—then it's possible to transform average or even poor performers into highly productive people.

In fact, while top performers are important, I think it's a bad idea to focus exclusively on them. "A" students may be top performers in school, but that doesn't necessarily mean they are going to be successful, hold a job, and make good decisions.

If you invest in programs that improve the work environment and raise the performance bar, you can help everyone become a top performer. And performance is a prerequisite for building a productive, competitive organization. Together, performance and productivity are the gold standard of today's business climate. If your company is not productive, it will be overwhelmed and perhaps eliminated by a younger, more athletic company whose work environment does promote productivity and performance for all.

Leadership Makes the Difference

Leadership is the most critical factor in determining whether a company invests in creating a high-retention culture.

I called my company "Chart Your Course" because I believe businesses, like sailing ships, need a captain to keep them on course. It's up to the captain to keep his or her eye on the destination and direct the crew to carefully trim the sails for maximum performance, speed, and direction.

Leaders are more than just figureheads. In carrying out their responsibility of setting the direction, speed, and performance of the individuals within a company, they are ever-present: touching,

Responsibility for setting direction can't be delegated or left to a computer. Businesses that have replaced their leaders with technicians, their brains with a hard drive, are in for a rude surprise.

motivating, talking, and checking, barrier removing, training, preparing, breathing, active, moving about, and creating change. Responsibility for setting direction can't be delegated or left to a computer. Businesses that have replaced their leaders with technicians, their brains with a hard drive, are in for a rude surprise.

Leadership is responsible for everything the organization does or fails to do. It's up to leaders to scan the horizon for challenges, obstacles, and catalysts for change. They also need to look below the surface for problems within the ship. Leadership needs to listen to the crew below the deck, for they usually have the best ideas and solutions.

It's also up to leaders to keep an organization from becoming rigid, inflexible, and difficult to steer toward change. Course changes happen quickly. Leaders need to encourage the kind of communication that lets information flow freely to everyone on all decks, so that everyone knows what to do if a sudden course correction is required.

My nautical theme may sound old fashioned, but it's very pertinent today. A strong, effective leader is a prerequisite for a successful retention program. In fact, it can't be created without one. When the captain is invested in TRM, the crew will follow suit.

The Eight Elements of Talent Relationship Management

There are many ways to create a TRM culture. In my years as a consultant, I have identified eight basic elements that are essential. While each one, like the sails of a ship, can harness the power of the wind, all eight are needed to transform an organization. A sail that is not properly set or is missing hinders the ship and causes frustration among the crewmembers.

1. **A Clear Sense of Direction and Purpose**
   People want to be part of an organization that stands for something and gives them personal fulfillment and meaning. When an organization means something, people are willing to give more. That's why people work for non-profit organizations, or spend their off-work hours leading scout troops and building houses for Habitat for Humanity. Employers can create meaning and purpose, align employees with its mission, and nurture a more dedicated, productive, and profitable crew.

2. **Caring Management**
   Interpersonal skills are an essential element of the TRM culture. People want to feel that management cares and is concerned for them as individuals, yet poor "soft skills" are one of the biggest factors that drive people away. Leaders must create an environment that values relationships and people.

3. **Flexible Benefits and Schedules Adapted to the Needs of the Individual**
   In today's workplace, flexibility rules. One-size-fits-all approaches to benefits have long since lost their effectiveness. Workers will migrate to companies whose benefit packages and schedules help them meet the demands of their lives, whether they are single parents, adults who care for aging parents, older workers, younger workers, part-time workers, and telecommuters.

4. **Open Communication**
   In our technological age, people have a large appetite for information, and they want it instantly. TRM workplaces place high priority on delivering the right information to the right people at the right time using the right methodology. Companies that leave employees in the dark risk damaging morale and motivation—not to mention compromising their ability to make a quick course change in the marketplace.

5. **A Charged Work Environment**
   People want to enjoy their work. They shun boring, bureaucratic, lifeless work environments. That's why high-retention workplaces don't bother with the traditional ways of doing things. They find new ways to make work mentally engaging and physically energizing. They also ask for, listen to, and implement the ideas and suggestions of those who work for them.

6. **Performance Management**
   It is becoming increasing more difficult finding competent, motivated workers who have good attitudes and work ethics. Because of this knowing how to manage performance is much more important in creating a TRM workplace. Performance management includes a series of tools, techniques, and processes that can help align an individual and his or her behavior with the goals of the business enterprise.

7. **Reward and Recognition**
   All humans need to feel appreciated. Reward and recognition programs help meet that need. A positive workplace that rewards and recognizes people builds higher productivity and loyalty and can create consequences for desired behavior that leads to organizational success.

8. **Training and Development**
   Today's workers want opportunity. They want to develop their skills and potential and enhance their ability to contribute and succeed. Training and development gives people

A positive workplace that rewards and recognizes people builds higher productivity and loyalty and can create consequences for desired behavior that leads to organizational success.

greater control and ownership over their jobs, making them more capable of taking care of customers and creating better management-employee relationships.

SAS Institute: A Calm Ship in a Sea of Turbulence

An example of an organization that provides a holistic work environment is SAS Institute Inc., located in North Carolina's Research Triangle Park.

SAS resembles a college campus more than a software development company. Everything from the baby grand piano in the company cafeteria to the giant outdoor chess board gives clear indication that this is a world apart. *Fortune* magazine lists it as one of the "Top 100 Best Places to Work," and employees agree. Turnover hovers around 3.7 percent and has never exceeded 5 percent in its twenty years of existence. The national average for most industries is 15 to 20 percent. Many employees have loyalty stronger than any glue seen. One graphic designer routinely turns down job offers from Silicon Valley for as much as 40 percent more money.

Many people say working at SAS is like working with your family. Their 5,400 employees find a nurturing environment and in some cases is the closest thing to a real family than many people have experienced. The benefits and perks go beyond what most businesses are willing to do for their employees including:

Loyalty can't be bought by benefits and perks, but SAS appears to have created a workplace where employees know they are cared for, trusted, and treated like adults.

- Unlimited sick leave: There is no limit to how much sick leave employees can use. Bob Goodnight, SAS President, PhD and billionaire believes if you treat adults like adults they will act as adults. Whether you are out sick for six days or six months it is not a problem.
- On Site Daycare: For $250 a month, employees can place their children in the day-care facility. Parents are encouraged to eat lunch and dinner with their children. The company cafeteria is equipped with highchairs.
- Free Family Healthcare: In lieu of health insurance SAS staffs a medical clinic 24 hours a day for employees and their family members. This saves the company $300,000 a year in health insurance costs.
- Equal Pay for Equal Work: Many businesses run off good employees because new hires are able to start making higher salaries than the "old" employees. Not at SAS. If SAS has to hire new employees and pay them more, all employees with the same skills levels receive the same pay raise. The average salary is $50,000 a year.
- Thirty-five-Hour Workweeks: All employees work five seven-hour workdays. Everything closes up at 5 P.M.
- Break Areas & Free Food: Each floor has its own break area stocked with complimentary refreshments, including all the

> M&M's employees can eat. SAS spends $45,000 annually on twenty-two tons of the little chocolate candies.

Loyalty can't be bought by benefits and perks, but SAS appears to have created a workplace where employees know they are cared for, trusted, and treated like adults.

> "Anyone who stops learning is old, whether this happens at twenty or at eighty. Anyone who keeps learning not only remains young but becomes constantly more valuable, regardless of physical capacity."

—Henry Ford

3

Executive Coaching: Retention Tool in Uncertain Times

JEFFREY M. COHEN

Jeffrey M. Cohen, a New York-based executive coach and industrial/organizational psychologist for almost two decades, continues to raise the bar on the quality and efficacy of executive coaching in organizations. A pioneer in his field, Mr. Cohen's work in performance management has been praised by The Conference Board. Currently he is co-chair of a national committee of predominantly corporate development executives who are determining benchmarks in such areas as selecting coaches, as well as developing return on investment models for executive coaching. Mr. Cohen can be reached at jcohen5970@aol.com.

Sometimes disparate ideas just come together.

Last fall I was asked to make a speech by the Management Development Forum here in New York City about the future of Executive Coaching. Because I thought it was presumptuous of me to opine on such a complicated and controversial subject, I developed a phone survey of corporate human resources generalists and management development specialists as well as a few thought-leaders in Executive Coaching. The purpose of the interviews was to get the pulse of the direction coaching was taking in the wake of September 11th. The results were at first surprising and then upon reflection and some additional reading made sense. First, the almost unanimous consensus was that Executive Coaching was needed now more than ever. In light of the fragility of the rank and file (especially here in New York) and the extra demands that were being placed on executives (defined here as those who manage managers), there is a necessity to assist those leaders who, on one hand, are expected to emotionally support their staff and keep a "stiff upper lip" while, on the other hand, are also expected to drive the business as if nothing had happened. A number of firms, especially those in the financial service community, revealed they were cutting their overall training budget but were planning to increase their expenditure for coaching, at least in the near term. As one development manager put it, "These managers are like blotters. They're absorbing all the anxiety that surrounds them. . . . They need our help."

Six months later I led a panel discussion on the topic of "Executive Coaching: The Good, The Bad, The Ugly" for New York Human Resources Planners. I did another mini-survey (with a smaller, different sample) and asked similar questions and received remarkably congruent response. The respondents concluded that Executive Coaching was still on the ascendancy, despite some concerns about the proliferation of coaches.

Other conclusions of my phone survey were very understandable and in retrospect aided me in explaining the first conclusion that Executive Coaching was on the rise. Here, the survey participants concluded that the primary functions of a Human Resources department should continue to be attracting and retaining the best talent. Essentially, the HR function needs to stay close to their knitting and concentrate on the basics when in ambiguous times.

I also inferred that the HR functional emphasis appears to lean somewhat toward the retention side of the equation. Organizations know they need to retain their potential leaders of the future—a commodity that is rather short supply. More and more companies such as Colgate are spending considerable dollars and attention, including the COO's and CEO's time, to assure there is a legacy ready to step into leadership roles.

Reflecting further on the survey, it appears the selection side of the equation had been getting much of the attention over the last few years and seems to have been aided much more by technology. The sophisticated HR practitioner has now turned to new technologies to foster the attraction and hiring of key employees.

Such technologies are not only cost effective for the HR practitioner in the timely tracking and screening of applicants, they are also appreciated by the candidate who is aware he/she is being moved through the labyrinth called the "selection system" by a cutting-edge company interested in combining the art form of selection techniques with the enhancements science makes possible.

The fact that employees know their company is on the cutting-edge boosts the image of the company. In turn, it buttresses the firm's retention strategy and, as such, it is a critical building block in having employees feel positively toward their company. It is the first step in retaining employee and maintaining their motivation.

The data I collected, that Executive Coaching was on the rise and that attraction and retention remain HR's focus, came together for me when I surfing the net looking for information I could use for a committee meeting I was attending. I came across an article in Onvia.com on supervisory practices. It stated that the number one reason (by far) for employees to leave their employer is caused by their direct supervisor. The fact that poor supervision was critical to voluntary turnover was easy to fathom, but the percentage of turnover it accounted for was for me astounding:

> Eighty percent of workers who voluntarily quit a job do so because of problems with their immediate supervisor.

According to the Saratoga Institute, a Santa Clara, California consulting company that specializes in human resources, that figure has been consistent for the last fifteen years that Saratoga has conducted exit interviews and surveys with more than 60,000 employees, across all sectors and sizes of companies. The results indicate that it's not about money. It's more likely about lack of supervision, lack of direction, no performance review, and long hours. Then it comes down to, "How well am I being paid for this?" The answer is often, "Not well enough." (Onvia.com)

Saratoga Institute indicated the cost to replace professional employees could be equivalent to a full year's salary, with benefits, when lost time and training are factored in. For lower positions, the cost is approximately half a year's salary.

That's a big financial hit, but poor managing was often overlooked in the past as the primary trigger in an employee's decision to leave. That's where I think that Executive Coaching comes in. By helping a manager do his job better, coaching can help stem employee turnover.

Attracting and retaining talent doesn't happen under bureaucratic leadership. Intelligent leadership's aim is to release the initiative and brainpower of workers.

Experts say the burden of proof falls on the manager to guide and even inspire employees, while making sure jobs are well defined with growth potential. In leadership terms, this means getting the best out of people by empowering them, supporting them, and getting out of their way. Attracting and retaining talent doesn't happen under bureaucratic leadership. Intelligent leadership's aim is to release the initiative and brainpower of workers. Employees will remain with companies where they are being stretched, where they can learn, and where they are being appreciated. As a colleague of mine, George Hollenbeck (2002) put it, there is a "new workforce with new wants and desires, operating within new social and economic arrangement in a world characterized by technological change and increasing globalization, requiring that business and people be managed differently." Executives were required to be coaches rather than continue in the old command-and-control style. Organizations such as JP Morgan Chase want to change the model of management so as to expeditiously transition to this new order and retain their key people as well provide a live model (the Executive Coach) for their executives to follow.

My presumption is: Executive Coaching not only assists in transforming behavior, but also has an impact on retaining those below the executive being coached. Among the reasons why Executive Coaching has had (and apparently will continue to have) such broad appeal is that it may actually be more efficient than traditional management development programs in facilitating managerial change of day-to-day behavior. The kind of transformations that attract employees—not drive them away.

We all know how difficult it is to make a significant change. We usually either must experience a life altering event (close relation dies, a heart attack) or assistance from someone (from a financial planner to a personal trainer) to help us make modifications in our lives. With Executive Coaching a rifle shot approach is taken: those who need the support receive just-in-time, one-on-one training.

Executive Coaching is not for everyone—for example, the coachee must want to change. Maybe even more importantly, there must be a business necessity to bring in a coach.

Its wide use makes sense. Richard Kilburg in his book, *Executive Coaching: Developing Managerial Wisdom in a World of Chaos* (1999), says that executive coaching plays a central role in enabling individuals, teams, and organizations to develop capacities. Manchester Consultants has shown Executive Coaching interventions to be statistically significant related to the bottom line. Many forward-thinking companies that are using coaches state in their internal literature that the process has increasingly been able to help their managers become even more valuable to their company.

Why is it such a timely fit for HR's retention concerns? Probably because its result are real-world, real-time oriented. There are no role playing or far-fetched exercises involved. Beth O'Neill's book *Executive Coaching with a Backbone and a Heart* (2000) is a typical blueprint for the approach that more experienced coaches might take. It's pragmatic (i.e., a backbone) and yet it encourages empathy (i.e., a heart). She proposes good probing and confronting questionings along with four essential ingredients make a foundation for good coaching of executives. The four ingredients are:

1. Having a results orientation to a leader's problem (*"What business challenges are you facing? How much time have you got?"*). A coach's job is to have a mission paralleling the leader's drive for results.

2. The second ingredient is partnership where the coach becomes a partner in the executive's journey toward greater competence and effectiveness.

3. The third ingredient is the ability to engage the executive in the specific leadership challenges he faces ("What is challenging for you in this situation . . . ?").

4. In the fourth ingredient, the coach links team behavior to the bottom-line goal, and points out the need for the executive to set specific expectations of their teams to achieve results.

The above indicates that Executive Coaching is not viewed by my colleagues as touchy-feely or new age ideas that make us feel good while we're participating but have us asking, "Where's the beef?" upon reflection. Because we all need to move with quickness and agility, we require a training process that is centered on results, lasting, easy to absorb, and makes sense in a fast-paced workplace. John Kotter of the Harvard Business School commented on the growth and usefulness of coaching stated: "As we move from thirty miles an hour to seventy to 120 to 180 . . . as we go from driving straight down the road to making right turns and left turns, to abandoning cars and getting on motorcycles . . . the whole game changes, and a lot of people are trying to keep up and learn how not to fall off." (From Hollenbeck, p. 5).

Coaching makes good sense to executives. Intuitively we know that executive are at times self-absorbed. They don't want to be part of the rest of the company's development training "program." They want their own. That's another reason why one-on-one guidance has the appeal (and 'cache') to assist them in making the changes that are required during these uncertain times.

It takes months, not a one-day quick fix, to assist executives who may wish to alter their modus operandi. Change that is sustainable and dependable under stress requires consistent encouragement, practice, and feedback. Complex behavioral changes also need time to develop, time to be tested in action, and time to be refined. Development occurs when its authentic, in relationship with others, and within context. It's part of a quality, long-term Executive Coaching relationship that includes:

1. **Awareness and ownership** of the need for change
2. **Action** taken to effect change
3. **Repeated action** and practice in real-world situations
4. **Feedback** that is trusted and accurate (from peers as well as coach)
5. **Time** for new habits to develop
6. **Skilled coaching** in recognizing competing values and commitments as well as underlying assumptions and governing variables to mental models (From *Coaching Matter,* Volume III, Number 5)

Executive Coaches help managers to develop skills of self-observation, self-awareness, self-responsibility, and self-mastery.

These skills allow managers to continue their growth long after the coaching relationship ends. Good coaches provide thought-provoking questions and assignments to help managers maximize their unique talents. Coaching develops extraordinary leaders. Extraordinary leaders produce extraordinary results and keep their staff motivated and happy. And extraordinary business results working through our employees is what we need *now*.

Bibliography

Hollenbeck, George, *Coaching Executives: Individual Leader Development* (manuscript to be published in Silzer (ed) The 21st Century Executive, 2002).

Kilburg, Richard, *Executive Coaching: Developing Management Wisdom in the World of Chaos* (1999).

O'Neill, Beth, *Executive Coaching with a Backbone and a Heart* (2000).

> "To find what one is fitted to do, and to secure an opportunity to do it, is the key to happiness."

—John Dewey

3

Rehabilitating the Problem Employee

LAWRENCE M. BIENATI PhD

Lawrence M. Bienati PhD is the President of Consultants to Management and has over twenty years senior level experience in numerous organizational settings. He teaches in the Management, Law, and Graduate Health Services Program at Saint Mary's College and is also part-time adjunct faculty at UC Berkeley where he teaches the human resources certification courses and leadership courses. A respected professional speaker, author, and consultant in many areas of human resources including employee relations law, executive compensation, and strategic planning, Dr. Bienati can be reached at bienati@onestophr.com.

The Challenge of Progressive Discipline

There is nothing more difficult in management than dealing with a problem employee. The author's research found 10 percent of the employees in a given organization contribute to 80 percent of the performance problems. Despite this minimal influence, successful organizations establish the right policies, procedures, and management practices to prevent frivolous litigation at all levels.

Another challenge faced by many managers is miscoding a "problem employee" from an "employee with a problem." It is a very distinct behavioral problem when you have an individual who is an otherwise good performer who, for some reason, is going through a performance decline. In these cases, the issue may not be one of problem behaviors; rather, issues outside of the work environment that may be impacting his or her current work performance. Employee Assistance Programs (24-hour, 7 day-a-week support services for employees) have grown markedly over the last twelve years. Successful managers find that the Employee Assistance Program is typically a positive first step before going through the pains and labors of progressive discipline systems.

The dictionary definition of discipline is to correct and train an individual's behaviors. Most organizations employ the traditional discipline process when dealing with a problem employee. We know the model as counseling, verbal warning, written warning, final written warning, suspension, and termination. It is the author's experience that these systems tend to operate on a philosophy of "trying to get the employee progressively better by treating them progressively worse." Sometimes the threat of discipline creates a significant emotional event that leads to a short-term awareness factor. This effect of "motivating by fear" may be effective in the short term, but rarely produces meaningful long-term improvement in employee performance.

In addition, most progressive discipline systems outline the problem behavior, identify the specific policy and procedure violations, and then culminate in a tight paper trail. These systems lack a meaningful program of correction and emphasis on rehabilitation in the employee performance profile. It is no wonder that there are emerging torts in the area of negligent supervision, negligent evaluation, and breach of a covenant of good faith and fair dealing. All of these emerging tort theories suggest that there is a duty owed on the part of a manger to provide a "good faith effort" and "due process" requirements to improve employee performance.

Beyond the legal documentation, there are other reasons for wanting to rehabilitate the problem employee. First, companies have an ethical duty to treat employees fairly and within the respectful boundaries of statutory law. Second, organizations should realize that there is a huge investment in employee replacement costs; letting a five to ten year employee go can lead to additional expenses in hiring, developing, and outplacement costs. Studies conducted by the author show a significant dollar payback in a performance action plan process, given the amount of money and time invested in an employee. Third, there is a social cost. Many of the behaviors we see include violence in the workplace; i.e. employees retaliating against supervisors, can be traced to some form of unfairness or insensitive

The PAP is a living document created by mutual understanding and agreement by a manager and an employee.

approach in the handling of their employee relations experience. One can compare the loss of job to a form of economic capital punishment. When you deprive an individual of life, liberty, and pursuit of happiness, he may have nothing to lose. Emotional triggers could lead to egregious actions against you, the supervising manager.

Taken collectively, it is the author's opinion that there is a duty owed to treat employees with the level of respect, fairness, and due process in any organization. This process, known as the Performance Action Plan (PAP), is not for organizations that use reengineering, layoffs, or reduction in force as a quick and simple way of solving their performance problems. The PAP is a vehicle for organizations who desire to create a culture that is built to last; a culture of low turnover, high productivity, high employee satisfaction. These cultures believe that management and employees should work together toward achieving the company's vision. Good leaders are coaches. They accept diversity and varied employee skill sets as a sign of balanced organizational strength. Mentoring is one of the top five management task areas.

Admittedly, there are some personnel events that are not conducive to the PAP. When an employee engages in misconduct, or other egregious actions that violate company policies and procedures, it is generally not necessary to follow all process steps of correction. The nature of the infraction, the employee's work history and the threat posed to the company are generally strong enough to sustain a termination. Life, however, is not that simple. One will find that a majority of separations in this country tend to fall within a "planned separation event." In a planned separation event, there is some form of due process or minimal warning that should take place before an individual is terminated from the organization. These planned events may constitute about 90 percent of most terminations in organizations.

This paper presents the following: 1) a new and enlightened approach to correcting problem employee performance; 2) a practical model where the steps of progressive discipline are a thing of the past; 3) a concept that blends the job description system, the performance appraisal process, proven training and development tools, and the communication of mutual expectations into a living document to rehabilitate problem employee behaviors. Let's proceed.

What Is a Performance Action Plan?

A performance action plan (PAP) is a blending of the best practices of progressive discipline systems with the best practices of employee training and development. The PAP is a supplement to the performance appraisal process. The PAP is a living document created by mutual understanding and agreement by a manager and an employee. The document captures: 1) issues of performance concern; 2) examples of behaviors that need to be corrected; 3) a road map; and, 4) specific action steps and milestones for correction. In most action plans the organization provides external and internal resources to help the employees succeed.

The organization is accountable to provide the training support, remove obstacles as appropriate, and coach employee performance to minimum acceptable levels. The employee, on the other hand, is accountable to achieve the specific actions, timelines, and deliverables established within the performance action plan. Once the action plan is created, a significant accountability is placed on the employee. In the author's use of over 200 action plans since 1989, he found that many employees appreciated the depth and quality of the performance action plan process. It is a sad fact that in most organizations, many employees do not receive a job description, new employee orientation programs or the types of communication to understand how to succeed within their jobs and their respective culture. Some of the individuals who succeed in the performance action plan process say it was their first time, while employed, that they actually had a document that established the expectations of desired performance. It is, therefore, not a successful practice of management to wait until the event of discipline to communicate expectations. It is failure of management!

What Lessons Have We Learned In Developing Successful Action Plans?

The concepts presented in this paper reflect the doctoral research and practice of the author, Larry Bienati, a HR practitioner and consultant over eighteen years. For additional insight and reference to the depth of performance action plans you may want to reference his dissertation entitled, "Salvaging the Problem Employee: A Critical Evaluation of Alternative Organizational Methods." This dissertation may be obtained through UMI at 1.800.521.0600, order number 9207650. Web site: www.onestophr.com.

The author found the following in his research on performance action plan process:

1. **Culture Drives the Process.** This finding suggests that if you are in an organization that has a very low tolerance for allowing an individual the appropriate time to correct problem behaviors, then it is not worth your time and effort to engage in the performance action plan process. In these cultures

where time, money, and patience is lacking, the organization is better served to go through other forms of employee separation or transitional packages, even the traditional progressive discipline systems.

2. **The Role of an Organizational Mentor.** The research suggests that mentoring is key to the rehabilitation process. This mentor (or support person) may not be the direct manager. Therefore, strong consideration should be given to identifying an individual within, or outside the organization that could serve as a coach/sounding board for the development of specific skill areas.

3. **The Approach to Presentation.** It was a statistically significant finding that the manner in which discipline is approached is critical to the rehabilitation process. An action plan that is forced on an employee generally does not work. An action plan where the employee is allowed to participate and discover problem areas and suggested correction steps led to successful outcomes. If an individual does not understand, accept, and commit to the problem performance behaviors, then the action plan process is an event in futility. When an individual feels involved and empowered to offer input into how the corrections should occur, the results are far more advantageous.

4. **Frequency of Performance Communication.** Action plans have a lower likelihood of success if an individual has not received the appropriate performance appraisals in the time preceding the delivery of the action plan. If an individual is just "hit from the blue" after thinking for years he or she has performed to expectation, then the acceptance factor could be far less. If there is lacking documentation, or a lacking of orientation or training program for the employee, it may take additional time to effect the rehabilitation process.

5. **Recognition that Certain Behaviors May Not be Changeable.** This subject is beyond the scope of this paper,

and individuals are encouraged to refer to "The Guide to Developing Management and Employee Skills" (linkage on this web-site at www.onestophr.com). Certain behaviors may not be changeable within a 90-day timeframe. These behaviors include: problem solving, problem analysis, decisiveness, initiative, innovation, risk taking, personal impact stress tolerance. These behaviors are changeable, but may require additional time and more on-line direct mentoring with the employee. Other behaviors, however, such as style of management, communication skills, time management, delegation, technical training, and other interpersonal skills can be corrected if:

- the individual accepts there is a problem
- there is a program of correction, and
- there is an on-the-job follow up on measurement and accountability.

6. **The Value of Outside Training.** It was another interesting research finding to note that individuals who were given the opportunity to balance internal training programs with external training programs, tended to fair better in action plan success. Specifically, when an individual participates in outside training seminars with individuals from other organizations, he or, she may discover that things may not be as bad at the home office. Also, outside training lends additional understanding and a sense of perspective for the employee.

7. **Remove Obstacles.** You have two choices: 1) wait and find out at the trial through the plaintiff's attorneys questioning, or 2) identify the obstacles at the onset of the PAP and try to eliminate them so the employee can succeed in the rehabilitation process. It is an interesting note that most corrective action plans fail to address what obstacles are currently impeding the employee's current level of performance. It is

critical to identify the obstacles during the setup and administration of an action plan. Be sure to manage the challenges that can be controlled versus those that cannot be controlled. Documenting these behaviors as a part of the action plan document will prevent a potential litigation for a breach of a covenant of good faith and fair dealing. It will show that the employer took a genuine interest in the employee's success.

8. **If it Cannot be Measured, It Cannot be Evaluated.** It is very important in the action plan process to establish specific dates, measurements, responsibilities, and accountabilities among the principal parties in the employee correction process. Action plans that are laced with goals versus objectives tend to be far less successful. An action plan that possesses "good objectives" tends to specify the "what, when, and how of a specific performance development."

9. **Patience.** The action plan process takes time. It is important to develop an action plan with incremental victories at the onset and then develop more successive benchmarks. It is an exercise in futility to have twelve developmental areas—all requiring correction within thirty days. Most action plans focus on three to four specific performance areas and provide ongoing mentoring and weekly reviews to measure progress.

10. **It Is a Memorandum of Understanding.** Performance action plans to be effective must outline two things: 1) what will happen to the employee if performance improves? 2) what will happen if performance does not improve? It is critical at the end of the performance action plan document to specify what steps the company will take at the various milestones if performance does not improve. This is an area of management that we are all uncomfortable with, specifically, having to tell an individual that their job could be in peril.

How to Develop a Successful Performance Action Plan

In the next section the author will outline a theoretical process for an action plan. The author will approach the discussion in a paragraph-by-paragraph format and then provide a working example of the concept. This will then culminate in a sample action plan that can be used as a model for your needs. Here are some of the lessons learned in developing a successful action plan:

1. **Approach the action plan as a letter of understanding.** It is usually more effective to have an action plan support the performance appraisal form. The beauty of a performance appraisal is that it clearly outlines the skill areas of successful job performance. The form also provides indications for where the development areas occur along with specific behaviors. One option, therefore, is to attach a performance action plan to the performance appraisal form. Another option is to prepare the action plan in a memorandum format, basically addressing it to the employee from the company with the subject entitled, "Performance Action Plan for the Period January xx to April xx."

2. **The first paragraph of the action plan should outline the steps that have preceded this process to rehabilitate employee performance.** This action plan may be key evidence for a jury someday. Your intent, of course, is to not reach this point if at all possible. If you do, you can feel assured that due process and proper documentation are on your side. Here is an example of a beginning paragraph for a performance action plan.

   John, this performance action plan is being prepared in an effort to help you achieve the minimum level of performance in your position. As you know, we have had discussions on this issue dating back over a year ago (dates). We also discussed some of these growth areas in your performance appraisal (dates) and other counseling discussions (dates). We have reached a point where these specific behaviors, with respect to your work performance, need to be corrected. Previous approaches were not as successful; therefore, this action plan represents a good faith effort on the part of the company to clearly identify these challenging behaviors and provide you with the necessary roadmap for correction.

Our intent is to help you succeed in your position within this organization. We have invested the appropriate time, energy, and dollar resources to help you in this action plan. We will outline where some of the challenging performance issues exist by providing specific examples of what is expected. We will then take each one of these skill areas and identify on-the-job and off-the-job ways that you will be able to correct this skill. We will then establish specific milestones and responsibilities on the part of both you and the company in measuring our progress toward correcting these areas. We will then formalize our understanding of the expectations of achieving and not achieving the action plans.

This action plan represents the best thinking on the part of the organization to help you succeed. We would like you to take our ideas and suggestions and spend a day or two reviewing them. We would like your input and involvement in the steps that we could take toward developing these skill areas. Our goal is to have the action plan ready for implement by (date).

If you do not want to participate in this action plan process, or feel that the approach we have outlined is not conducive to your expectations, then we will have to meet and discuss alternative methods for handling some of these performance difficulties. We hope you will consider this action plan process. We are, however, fully prepared to evaluate other alternatives at this time.

3. **Once you have clearly identified the history of the performance challenge and then given the employee a choice**

of participation, you can proceed to outline the problem skill behaviors. This section of the action plan reflects the specific behaviors that need to be corrected. For example:

- managing multiple priorities
- following through on specific performance tasks
- improving client relationship skills
- improving management skills
- improving time management skills
- developing an increased technical awareness of position requirements

These skills clearly are not inclusive of all the different skill sets; it is presented for example purposes only. Successful action plans will take each one of these skill areas and write a sentence or two to explain the specific behavior that needs to be corrected. For example, in the area of delegation you may write, "tends to try and do too much work himself; does not capitalize on the many opportunities to assign tasks to employees."

The key to this section is ensuring that you have a behavior or example to support the skill that needs to be corrected. If you are at a loss for determining what behaviors to place here, you should refer to the "Guide to Developing Employee Management Skills," by Bienati. In this guide, he not only identifies the skill but also identifies measurable problem behaviors along with programs for correction. Remember that an action plan is a form of due process. Avoid meaningless generalities or vague statements that cannot be supported in the future should you be questioned as to what specific performance problems occurred. If you are conducting performance appraisals on a regular basis, you should have enough of a performance basis and background to substantiate these problem behaviors.

4. **The next step of the action plan is focused on taking each one of the skill areas that need to be corrected and then developing the appropriate training solutions.** The training solution will clearly differ by skill area. You are encouraged to review the "Guide to Developing Employee and Management Skills" or the "Manager's Handbook" by Development Dimensions International. These two guides will give you some excellent on-the-job versus off-the-job ways of correcting a specific skill area.

It is important when you develop this section of the action plan to be specific. For example, let's say that an individual needs to strengthen his ability in managing multiple priorities. Your training solution might be:

Attend the Franklin Time Management seminar no later than (date). After attending the seminar, prepare a one- to two-page document that clearly outlines the specific actions you will take to improve this area. Be prepared to present this to your manager for discussion, review, and measurement over the ensuing sixty days.

In addition to attending the Franklin Time Management seminar, we also suggest that you consider an on-the-job action plan. We provide a sample checklist of things that you might consider to improve your time management skills. These include:

- *Establish a to-do list every morning you begin your job*
- *Assign specific priorities to task areas*
- *Manage phone conversations and stay focused on the issues*
- *Focus on one task at a time*
- *Perform routine mail and administrative duties during early morning, afternoon, or late evening hours*

- *Allow for slack in your schedule to accommodate unforeseen contingencies, etc.*

So, in essence, each skill area has a specific training solution with a measurement and a review point by the manager and employee.

A specific training solution is then developed for each one of these skill sets. It is not uncommon that some of these skill sets may integrate with each other. If this is the case, ensure that the training solution, timelines, and measurements do not conflict with each other.

5. **Identify obstacles.** This part of the action plan process occurs after you have presented the first four sections to the employee. Research has found that it is more effective to present the issues, identify the training solutions, and allow an individual a day or two to review the suggested corrective approach. While reviewing the corrective approach, you are asking the employee to return and identify the types of organizational obstacles that may impede the performance of the action plan.

   The goal here is to clearly identify what obstacles can and cannot be controlled. Your goal is to remove as many obstacles before the action plan is put into effect. Some employees may return and say there are no obstacles. If this happens you should record in the action plan document that you allowed the individual x number of days to return with an obstacle analysis, and they concluded that there were none. Again, this documentation is critical to show good faith and due process.

   If obstacles are identified be sure to list the obstacles in the action plan and the appropriate solution the organization will take to solve it. If you can accommodate the obstacle, then do so and note for the record. If you cannot accommodate and have a good business reason, be sure state in for the record as well.

Sample obstacles could include: *A need to achieve a project deliverable to a client within thirty days.*

The employee's obstacle is that they are not able to achieve that client's project need while trying to attend seminars and correct these problem behaviors in this action plan.

You may then decide to modify a portion of the action plan or find a way to help the individual in managing the client deliverable. In some cases you may not be able to accommodate the employee request. You may be left with the option of encouraging the employee to do the best they can within the constraints that we all face in any organization.

6. **The last part of the action establishes the understanding of improvement.** Throughout the action plan, you have hopefully established milestones in meeting dates to measure the relative progress of skill developments. In this section you may decide to take the specific dates and highlight what the specific requirements will be for correction.

   You may go a step further by identifying what the specific actions will be taken if performance does not improve. A typical phrase might be:

   This action plan represents a good faith on the part of the company to help you achieve the minimum performance requirements in your position. We have outlined a program of correction and we appreciate your willingness to participate in this developmental process and improve your job performance. We are confident you will succeed. It is very important for you to meet the various deliverables, dates, and timelines. If you feel you cannot meet a date, be sure that your supervisor is aware of it and a decision will be made at that point in time. If you have a specific deliverable and you fail to notify the supervisor and not meet that date, that can constitute a performance infraction within the action plan. Failure to achieve the noted performance measures could lead to your separation from the company.

It is important to be aware of this mutual accountability in achieving development in these areas. If you are successful in meeting these minimum performance requirements, the company will establish a remedial support plan; if performance improves to meet and exceed level of expectation, this document may be removed from your file so that you can move forward with your position in the company. Good Luck.

What about Monitoring?

Confucious once said, "A fine tool is nothing accept in a skilled hand." As you progress through the action plan process, it is important to stay vigilant to your responsibilities and timelines. It is equally important to meet with the employees and coach them throughout the process. If they are starting to achieve gain, tell them so and reward their performance so that you can encourage more positive behaviors. If you notice that within the first week or two that they are not meeting the performance expectations, then meet and carefully identify the problem areas. Remind them that if performance does not improve, that it could lead to a separation of employment.

It is a big mistake to deliver an action plan, wait thirty or sixty days and then follow up on performance. Performance should be monitored daily and the individual should understand that continuous improvement is required.

Good luck on your journey. If you have any questions about action plans, having someone review it prior to implementation, or the types of training solutions one might consider, feel free to send us an e-mail at www.onestophr.com. One of our consultants will be glad to spend a couple of minutes with you to provide the coaching and/or mentoring you need for this invaluable process.

On a final note, it is said that the mark of a successful leader can

---

A successful leader can be measured not in how they lead or how they motivate people; rather, in how they have changed challenging performance situations and rehabilitated individuals to a higher level of performance achievement.

---

be measured not in how they lead or how they motivate people; rather, in how they have changed challenging performance situations and rehabilitated individuals to a higher level of performance achievement. Good leaders accept the positives with the not so positives. They respect the fact that there is diversity among their team. They understand that different situational styles of management will apply based upon the skill, the need, and the maturity of the individuals under their care and supervision.

Therefore, the litmus test of a good leader: Taking complex situations and finding the kernels of strength to enliven their performance abilities of their people; the lost art of building on positives and minimizing weaknesses. It can be one of the most satisfying journeys of your career.

Sample Action Plans

A sample action plan is included on the following pages. Admittedly, this action plan is very detailed and serves to reinforce some of the concepts we have presented in this earlier section. There are less formal examples of action plans and many of these can be obtained through visiting www.onestophr.com. You can tailor the action plans as appropriate.

PERFORMANCE ACTION PLAN #1 (Sample)

DATE:	January 15, 2002
TO:	Engineering Manager
FROM:	Principal in Charge
SUBJECT:	Performance Action Plan for the Period January 15, 2002 to April 15, 2002

The following action plan has been prepared to help you strengthen the requisite management skills required of a successful engineering manger. This action plan follows previous discussions held during the last three months regarding specific concerns of your general office management performance. As requested, I have surveyed key staff, made observations of general "unrest" of staff that seemed to center on the tardiness of personnel (annual) reviews. From these discussions and interviews, it was concluded that a great deal of concern existed regarding concerns of apathy, frustration, and resignation with key team members. The timeliness of annual reviews was cited as only one aspect of this concern. If not solved soon, the situation could lead to major morale and overall office performance problems. The staff respects you from the indications during the interviews and previous meetings. They want this office to succeed with all the support from corporate and my office in accomplishing this endeavor.

The following are specific management concerns:

1. **Leadership.** Displays passive leadership in technical and marketing activities.

2. **Delegation.** A perceived abdication of responsibility. Delegates without follow through and review.

3. **Follow Through.** A reported lack of follow up with both assignments taken on by yourself and the monitoring of your subordinates' assignments.

4. **Timely Decisions and Reviews.** Decisions tend to be put off on reviews, written reports, and proposals. Follow through is

extended for periods of time, creating a credibility gap not only within the internal office but also in the external environment.

5. **Work Sharing Activities.** A perception exists that you are not taking on a fair share of the workload in the technical and marketing areas.

In preparing this action plan, we are cognizant of the fact that this office is still in a high-growth mode. Underlying the concerns expressed by employees in my general observation, is a need to strengthen your administrative abilities. In particular, establish a system of goal setting, planning, organizing, delegation, and further accountability. Additionally, there may be areas where my assistance in the technical areas of the Region B market might be of value.

The action plan represents a good faith on the company's effort to help you develop the skills you need to succeed in an action plan. The goals and timetables listed in this action plan are ambitious yet achievable. In order to develop these administrative skills area, it will be necessary to integrate off-the-job training programs along with on-the-job programs of weekly accountability. The goal is to provide a mentoring base to help you better manage your time and focus on the critical priorities of your office.

Action Plan for Engineering Manager

SPECIFIC ACTION STEPS (Sample)

The following action steps are recommended to strengthen the above-noted management skills. This action plan is designed to provide guidance both on-the-job and off-the-job to strengthen the areas of leadership, delegation, follow through, timely decisions, planning, organizing, and employee-involvement activities. For ease of administration and understanding, the action plan will be presented in numerical format. Dates, time lines, and specific programs of accountability have been included to ensure that the commitment of any level, your level, and any type of corporate involvement is properly facilitated by all parties involved.

1. **Delegation.** Acquire the cassette/tape series "Successful Delegation" through Larry Bienati's office. In addition to reviewing these particular training tapes, it is recommended that you complete the workbook that is included in the cassette/tape series. These tapes have been an excellent source of training for managers who need to further develop their skills in assigning tasks to subordinates commensurate with their responsibilities and roles within the organization. Upon completing the review of the cassette/tape and the workbook, I would like you to prepare a two-page summary of the principles learned in the cassette/tape series. In this report, please specify what specific action steps you plan to take on the job to strengthen your skills in delegation and accountability with subordinates. A copy of this report should be sent to my attention no later than March 1, 2002. We will review this report at our first thirty-day review following implementation of the action plan.

2. **Planning and Organizing.** Contact Larry Bienati and make plans to attend the seminar offered through Fred Pryor entitled "Managing Multiple Priorities." This program will assist you in strengthening your skills in planning, organizing, and time management. Following this seminar, be prepared to present an action plan at either our thirty-day or sixty-day meeting. You will present what specific action steps you will take to better manage your time (i.e., in-basket, timely review, and submittal of proposals, timely review of performance appraisal, and other personnel-related issues, balance of time spent on managerial marketing, and technical tasks.)

3. **Personnel.** Review the video cassette "The Human Touch Performance Appraisal." This can be acquired through Larry Bienati's office and will provide some counsel regarding how to best conduct a performance appraisal and deal with the sensitive personnel issues. We will observe two of your performance reviews.

4. **Management Development.** As a follow up to the Management Development Program, prepare a short memorandum to my attention outlining the specific action steps you plan to take to achieve the two business and two personal goals you

established in the development program. We will review your specific action plans at our thirty-day meeting and measure your progress to date in achieving these goals. I will be there to provide continuing counsel and guidance to ensure successful completion of these goals.

5. **Marketing.** As outlined in previous discussions, we need to strengthen the marketing efforts within Office A. The recommended on-the-job action steps include:

   a. Have weekly marketing meetings with your staff and plan to arrive on time
   b. Take the lead in assigning goals and contacts
   c. Demonstrate participation by your willingness to take on a portion of the sales load
   d. Make a minimum of six marketing contacts per week
   e. Work independently on your share of load and complete all assignments you have taken on

   In setting up a system of marketing, follow through, accountability, and some method of review and control, it is critical to ensure that client opportunities are maximized. Be prepared to discuss at our first thirty-day review meeting the specific action steps you have taken in the area of marketing and communications, both in the internal and external environment. Plan on sending me copies of the minutes of your weekly marketing meetings listing specific action steps, person responsible, and time-line for completion. Also, provide your individual contacts outlined in (d) on a weekly basis.

6. **Technical Skills.** It is my goal to serve as a mentor and to provide on-the-job training to help you best manage your time along these management, marketing, and technical responsibilities in the environment. Until you feel comfortable with the specific requirements in the Region B market, please review each geotechnical report sent from your office. Admittedly, reading these types of reports, does pose an obstacle to the effective use of your time; however, call upon my resources to help you familiarize yourself to the geotechnical policies, practices, and procedures

unique to this marketplace. It is important to ensure that no documents sit no more than one day on your desk. Make decisions on technical issues immediately, and do not defer them for periods of time. (We all tend to forget, and this leads to skepticism of technical ability.) By taking the lessons learned in the tape "Successful Delegation" coupled with my on-the-job counsel, a system of delegating work assignments, monitoring progress, and ensuring deadlines are met, will ensure that your credibility is maintained both internal and external to the environment.

7. **Review.** In addition, it is also recommended that you send proposals for future work through my office for review, clarification, and comment. We can then ensure that proposals are consistent with competitive systems within the Region B market. This type of communication on proposals will serve as a solid on-the-job training tool to help you understand the peculiarity of this office. We will spend some time on our thirty-day review meeting to ensure that your basic knowledge of the technical aspects inherent in this market are fully understood. Most important, recognize that I am here to help you as a resource. If you have a question on the guidance of a decision, please feel free to call me, and I will give you the appropriate support you need.

8. **On-the-Job Development.** Review the Guide to Developing Management/Employee Skills developed by Larry Bienati. Outside of reading this document, I would suggest that you make reference to the following skill areas: initiative (page 2); problem-solving skills and administrative skills (pages 24-32). In this guide you will find a listing of specific on-the-job action plans and checklists that you can follow to strengthen these critical skill areas. Pay close attention to the areas of planning, organizing, goal setting and delegation. Prepare to discuss at our thirty, sixty, and ninety-day meeting the specific action steps you have taken to strengthen these particular skill areas. I will use these relevant checklists as a benchmark by which we can effectively judge your progress.

9. **Personal Support.** In order to balance the pressures that are likely to occur between family, work, and professional growth, you may find it prudent as a part of this action plan to contact our company's Employee Assistance Program (EAP). The

Employee Assistance Program will provide additional support should you need and any type of help in balancing the time management/stress management activities inherent in your position. It may, therefore, be prudent to undertake some level of training through the EAP to develop a better perspective on how to balance your time and improve many of the issues outlined within this action plan. Feel free to contact Larry Bienati if you need additional support and guidance on this issue.

10. **Leadership.** Review the leadership self-assessment checklist that is contained on page 10 of the Guide to Developing Management Skills. This checklist outlines the thirteen practice aspects of participative management. It will also serve as a basis of review for our thirty, sixty, and ninety-day meetings. Be prepared to discuss what types of programs you have put in place to each one of these question areas. If you use this checklist as a daily record of activities, it will ensure that all issues inherent in the planning, organizing, staffing, directing, and controlling aspects of the management equation are properly implemented on the job.

Obstacle Analysis

The employee did not identify any obstacles that would impede his success in the action plan. We will therefore proceed as planned with the schedules.

Commitment and Understanding

In closing, this action has been prepared to help you strengthen your skills in the problem-solving, administrative, and leadership role in your office. The office now is entering its second year in existence. In a short period of time we have experienced a significant growth in staff, and now the time has come to effectively manage activities. I have the confidence that you can succeed at this, and you have my full support. If time begins to slip away on a daily basis, I suggest you use the time log and begin to track where a majority of your time is spent. It is my hope that this structured program of training will help you develop the type of skills required of a successful engineering manager. Please feel free to review, add, delete and comment on any of the above-noted training recommendations.

We are confident that you can succeed in this action plan. If you are unable to meet the expectations listed in this action plan then the company will need to evaluate your continued role as a manager and level of responsibility in the company. This decision as to continued employment will be made no later than April 15, 2002.

ACKNOWLEDGMENT

I have read and understand the terms, covenants and conditions outlined in this action plan.

Engineering Manager	Date
Principal in Charge	Date
Larry Bienati (Mentor)	Date

PERFORMANCE ACTION PLAN #2 (Sample)

DATE:	June 1, 2002
TO:	Truman Clark, Marketing Manager
FROM:	V.P. Marketing
SUBJECT:	Performance Action Plan for the Period June 1, 2002 to September 1, 2002

This action plan has been prepared in an effort to strengthen your management skills in the position of Marketing Manager. We recognize that you display certain areas of strength with the regard to the technical requirements of the job; the continuing challenges rests with your management abilities. Specific areas of development include planning, organizing, staffing, directing, and controlling.

During the last nine-month period, the company has engaged in extensive training and development in order to help you achieve the requisite level of skill required of a successful manager. In order to facilitate this training and development, you attended the Management Leader Program. During this program, areas of improvement through self-appraisal and through other individuals within the Dalin Corporation included, on a consistent basis: 1) the need to communicate; 2) impatience; 3) behavior flexibility; 4) developing a more assertive style; 5) strengthening leadership techniques.

Following this seminar your supervisor, Alicia Sicora, along with consultant, Mr. Jerome, worked with you exclusively for a ninety-day period to help you develop in these areas. Despite these efforts, your general level of management performance was not reaching accepting levels. On November 9, 2002, you received a verbal warning. On December 4, 1996, you received a Step 2 corrective notification. Issues included in this corrective notification were: 1) keeping your staff informed; 2) displaying active listening skills; 3) not accepting responsibility for your own mistakes; 4) involving your subordinates in day-to-day issues affecting the department; 5) failing to explain to subordinates reasons behind specific tasks assigned to them, which led to their making unnecessary mistakes; 6) involving yourself with day-to-day business issues and refraining from any comments regarding the personal lives of your subordinates.

During the ninety days that followed the Step 2 corrective notification, meetings with yourself, Alicia Sicora, and Tracy Powell were held. On April 1, 2002, you were issued a final written warning. While improvement was made in certain specific areas, it was noted that the following were still negatively impacting your performance: 1) a lack of credibility that was addressed during the Management Leader Program was still hampering your ability to effectively manage the department; 2) a failure to provide accurate facts to fellow workers and assuming ownership for errors committed; 3) misrepresenting facts to individuals inside and outside the company; 4) lack of ability to keep issues concerning people or activities confidential.

The general issues of management style again began to surface. At the April 11 meeting, Larry Bienati, Employee Relations Manager, and Alicia Sicora openly discussed options with you. We presented a transition and outplacement package as an alternative. It was your decision at the April 11 meeting that you wanted to stay with the Dalin organization and were willing to engage in whatever remedial training efforts were available in order to strengthen your management style consistent with the Marketing Department's expectations.

Action Plan for Truman Clark

At this April 11, 2002 meeting we also discussed the preparation of a ninety-day Action Plan which would define specific standards of expectation in the noted developmental areas. The Action Plan was to be monitored by Larry Bienati and Alicia Sicora on a thirty-day basis.

In preparing this Action Plan, we called a second meeting and asked you to identify specific obstacles that existed in the exercise of your daily management tasks. We desired to eliminate these obstacles so you could succeed in the action plan.

The company is committed to your successful development and will engage in this last-step effort if it will help strengthen your management abilities. This Action Plan will set forth minimum standards of expectation. The initiative, the accountability and the responsibility are incumbent upon you. It should be understood that this Action Plan does represent Dalin's final effort to assist you in attaining the noted improvement. If you achieve the noted levels of expectation, you will remain in the position of Marketing Manager. If you do not abide by the terms, covenants and conditions noted, your employment with Dalin will be terminated at the end of the ninety-day period.

You will have three to five days to review the recommendations put forth. Please feel free to add, delete, and question any area before signing the Action Plan. Your concerns may be addressed to either Alicia Sicora or Larry Bienati.

We are hopeful that you will achieve success in this Action Plan.

I. Challenges and Obstacles

The following challenges and obstacles were identified by you on May 8, 2002, in a memorandum and meeting with Larry Bienati and Alicia Sicora. These obstacles were:

A. The ability to have regular communication with supervisor to discuss ongoing operations and future planning.

Action Taken:
Alicia Sicora stated that she planned to have Wednesday morning meetings on a biweekly basis in order to facilitate regular communication.

B. Communication between Redistribution, Merchandise Administrators, and Marketing concerning product information and maintaining the item filer for proper information.

Action Taken:
It was determined that biweekly meetings would be held with the various departments noted above to endure that proper communication and expectations are understood. Alicia Sicora was going to work with the other department managers to facilitate this process.

C. The need to be involved in planning or receive information on a change in operation prior to the change taking place.

Action Taken:
Alicia Sicora stated that she will make every effort to involve you in this process. This links with I.A. and will likely tie into the Wednesday meetings.

D. Transportation Department recognition. Most of our store calls are still after-the-fact when they have already been burned by a freight bill.

Action Taken:
There was a long discussion on the start-up nature of the Marketing Department. It was also understood that as a service organization, perhaps their tasks are somewhat reactive in nature. One challenge that lies ahead is to create a preventive environment and, through proper training and communication, change the belief system of operations personnel so that they feel comfortable dealing with the Marketing Department

in other than crisis situations. This process that will evolve over time; its success, however, is a function of the department establishing credibility and maintaining proper communications with operations personnel.

E. There is a cumbersome system for inventory control and billing flow for our transportation and warehousing and production controls.

Action Taken:
This issue was left somewhat open; however, Alicia Sicora basically stated that some file maintenance issues were being reviewed by members of the MIS Department and, hopefully, resolution to the problem would be reached shortly.

F. The phone system. Each person needs to have the capability of picking up all lines and putting calls on hold. Many people are being cut off with the current system and messages are not being received on overflow calls.

Action Taken:
Larry Bienati stated that he would advise Karen Riggs to look into the possibility of adding two or three more lines. Larry has met with Karen, and as soon as the upgrade is made to the current phone system, the appropriate lines will be brought into the department. This may not take place, however, until August 2002.

G. The noise level in the physical space being occupied by three people.

Action Taken:
Until upper management makes a decision regarding space at the General Office, no change can take place in the physical space allotted the department. Alicia Sicora did advise Truman that if an opportunity for additional space did present itself, his department would be given priority.

II. Action Plan Expectations

Expectations will be presented in four specific areas:

1. Communications
2. Management
3. Accountability
4. Human Relations

A. Communications

In order to strengthen your communication ability, the following actions both on and off the job are required:

1. You are to enroll in an assertiveness training seminar sponsored through the American Management Institute. Two weeks following the implementation of this Action Plan, you are to contact Faye Rappaport to schedule your attendance at this seminar. The seminar should be completed no later than August 1, 2002. Within seven days following the seminar, you are to prepare a two-page report summarizing the principles learned and specific actions that will be taken on the job to strengthen your assertiveness in dealing with others.

   It should be noted that one area of development rests with becoming more animated, more enthusiastic, and employing vocal variety techniques when communicating with others. As noted in the feedback from the Management Leader Program, your soft-styled demeanor is creating false perceptions of your sincerity and credibility. A more fluid, spontaneous style will enhance these areas.

   If you have specific questions of what to strengthen in terms of assertiveness perception, contact Larry Bienati within one week of receiving this Action Plan in order to clarify them.

2. In addition to the seminar on assertiveness, there are specific tapes on assertiveness and communication which are available through Carol Edwards. Please check with her for more information on the books and tapes available to strengthen this area.

B. **Management Style**

In order to strengthen your general management and leadership abilities, the following actions are required:

1. Meet with Karl Dole within the first thirty days of the Action Plan and review governing principles related to employee relations. This will include: review of performance evaluation policy, review of discipline policy and review of general office practices and procedures. In addition, it is also recommended that you contact Linda Sisk and meet with her to review general office hiring, recruiting testing, and general employment standards. This familiarization is critical so that proper personnel policies and procedures are consistently applied.

2. You are to review the handout from Larry Bienati entitled "Positive Reinforcement". This handout will offer various strategies and techniques for properly rewarding behavior and creating a productive work force. On August 1, 2002, you are to submit a report to Larry Bienati of no more than two pages in length summarizing which principles you have used in promoting an environment of positive reinforcement. In this report you are to provide examples of what does and does not seem to work and the types of techniques and strategies you will continue to use with your employees.

3. You are to review the handout entitle "Theory P Practical Management". This will serve as a guide for helping you identify the motivational hot buttons in your employees and applying them in your daily management style. After reviewing the handout, you are to write a one-paragraph assessment in each of the thirteen areas on the Self-Assessment Leadership Checklist and provide examples to support your on-the-job practice or identify what you will do to begin to practice this on the job. This checklist will serve as a barometer to Alicia Sicora and Larry Bienati at the end of the ninety-day period to see if you are actually applying these principles. The completed Self-Assessment

Checklist should be submitted to Alicia Sicora for her review no later than July 15, 2002.

4. Acquire the Team Building tapes from Faye Rappaport. You are to complete the cassette tape series and the report book no later than August 15, 2002.

5. Within the first sixty days of this Action Plan and as a result of your weekly staff meetings, you are to actively involve your staff in achieving four business goals. In establishing these goals, you should use the what, when, how, why format. This will serve as an excellent problem-solving exercise in creating a participative management style. You should indicate specific time frames for how these goals will be achieved. Prior to implementation, the goals should be presented to Alicia Sicora for her approval. The successful completion of these goals will be reviewed at the end of this ninety-day Action Plan.

6. Read The Effective Executive by Drucker no later than July 20, 2002, and submit a two-page report to Larry Bienati identifying how you will apply certain principles in this book to your management style.

C. Accountability

Part of successful management requires that a manager set up programs to properly review, evaluate, and ensure accountability for task completion. Part of this issue of accountability and management control requires that subordinates be kept informed on daily policies, practices, and procedures affecting the department. This information should be communicated so that subordinates understand fully and clearly what is expected of them. No directive should be assumed, and proper confirmation or understanding should take place.

As noted earlier, this appears to be a developmental area. In your absence there is often confusion when subordinates do not understand what specific actions or activities are under evaluation and are likely to surface in your absence. Through your weekly meetings and through some form of accountability, you will have to ensure that in your absence all parties fully understand and are prepared to deal with the department's daily activities.

In order to do this, you are to develop a plan of action that will ensure proper communication, accountability, and definition of departmental standards. We will leave the format to your discretion; however, we would recommend that it be negotiated through a participative endeavor with your employees.

Coincident with developing this accountability mechanism, you are to complete the workbook/cassette program entitled "Successful Delegation," which is available from Larry Bienati. This program should be completed no later than August 1, 2002. These tapes should provide insight into developing your ability to delegate assignments using proper techniques.

D. Human Relations

One aspect of this Action Plan that has been brought out is the level of perception you have created among subordinates, peers, and outside vendors. You must make significant improvement in terms of your vendor relations skills. It has been reported that your "too demanding" style is tending to create an adversarial relationship with these critical sources. It is suggested that a more collaborative, cooperative style be used.

While there are many books available on the subjects of human relations and sensitivity, you are to develop your own personal checklist or philosophy which you will begin to employ in creating a more positive, open environment of vendor relations. This progress will be reviewed at the end of this Action Plan.

Another area requiring professionalism requires that you focus on day-to-day business issues with your employees. Previous reference has been made to your intruding into the personal lives of certain employees with individuals outside of the company. In order to maintain an environment of proper decorum and professionalism, you must use better discretion and judgment in your daily management of people.

Another area requires that your general relationships with other managers—Mimi Ford and Damon Whelchel, specifically—be improved. It is hoped that the biweekly meetings will serve as a basis for creating greater levels of teamwork. A perception has been created regarding both your management style and your general level of competence, truthfulness, and accuracy of statements. We do not expect each party to have to maintain documentation in order to protect their interests; rather, we expect all parties to get together and work out any concerns, solicit ideas, and suggestions, and work toward the company's objectives. The development of this style of communication will be monitored on a continual basis by Alicia Sicora.

Commitment and Understanding

Having read this Action Plan, it is recommended that you develop a time-line to list the actions required and their target dates, as well as note specific actions that must be taken to achieve the noted development. This time-line should be available for review by Alicia Sicora and Larry Bienati no later than one week following your signing this Action Plan.

Additionally, if there are other areas you wish to strengthen or for which you would like training materials or assistance, you should contact Faye Rappaport, who will serve as the general facilitator for this Action Plan.

As previously noted, this Action Plan will serve as a final corrective notification. We are hopeful and confident that you will achieve the requisite skill level required in a managerial position at Dalin. If you do not meet the terms, covenants, and conditions of this Action Plan, your employment will be separated at the end of the ninety-day period.

> "I never failed once.
It happened to be a
2000-step process."

—Thomas Edison

3

TRM's Number 2 Dilemma

ED NEWMAN

Ed Newman has more than fifteen years of experience in Human Resource Management with the last eleven years specializing in recruiting and the successful implementation of various recruiting software systems. He is the Founder and President of The Newman Group, a best practice consulting firm specializing in the implementation of recruiting technology. Mr. Newman was the Director of Employment and Corporate Human Resources at PRC in Mclean, VA. He has helped over 100 clients including such prestigious firms as Accenture, EMC, Coca-Cola, Johnson & Johnson, McKesson, SAP America, and the Walt Disney Company focus on using solid recruiting principles while leveraging technology. Mr. Newman can be reached at ed.newman@tngconsulting.com.

As an HR Generalist for a large Government contracting firm, one of my main responsibilities was recruiting and employment. In the professional services industry every new hire means direct labor, which translates into revenue for the company. It was as if the employment aspect of the job is what funded the rest of the position. As a recruiter I particularly enjoyed making the great hire. What is a great hire? It is when a candidate comes along who has the potential to do great things for the company for a long time. They have reasonable compensation expectations, and I place them in a job that is challenging and rewarding, working for a good manager who is very appreciative of the work I have done as a recruiter. One of the most painful aspects of my job was conducting the exit interview for one of those great hires.

The HR department in a high turnover industry, like government contracting, handles an abnormally high number of employment and termination transactions. In a given year I may have been personally responsible for hiring 100 new employees, but I may also have conducted seventy exit interviews. This may seem high to some people, but in Government contracting it is fairly normal. Contracts come and contracts go. When you win one you are faced with frantic hiring goals, but when you lose one, you need to help a bunch of people find jobs elsewhere. There was work inside the company for most, but there was always a percentage that you had to let go. And then there was the percentage that left when they saw the writing on the wall. These are the good ones, the great hires. They would get snatched up by a competitor with a blink of an eye. Like a good HR organization we tabulated and collated the exit interview data to see where we might improve our company. We were obviously most interested in the voluntary terminations and the reasons for them. Over my career as an HR professional I have found the most common reasons for voluntary terminations to be lack of promotion opportunities, transfer opportunities, and/or growth opportunities. Twelve years ago it didn't matter much because there was another bunch of candidates waiting to be hired. Now that we sit in one of the tightest labor markets in history, companies are really struggling to solve their retention problems.

As I take an objective look back at my experiences as an HR professional and an employee who has changed jobs on average every three to four years, I begin to see a pattern in retention that may shed some light. Corporate America is suffering from what I call "TRM's Number 2 Dilemma."

The Number 2 Dilemma

Most corporate HR departments are responsible for administering the performance review process, which includes some sort of appraisal form as well as an overall performance ranking. The traditional approach will have five different rankings where "one" far exceeds expectations, "two" exceeds expectations, "three" meets expectations, "four" needs improvement, and "five" is unsatisfactory. Terminology may vary, but it is normally five and there is often a recommended (and sometimes forced) distribution for managers when they rate their employees. For example, no more than 5 percent of an organization should be given a number one ranking. I am not necessarily against this type of system, however, I have noticed the TRM impact can have on an organization.

Please excuse the generalization, but with this type of system the number five's were just fired, the number four's will be gone tomorrow because they know they will be fired and are looking for a new job, the three's are fat and happy, the number one's are in the most exciting jobs in the company (and always will be), and the number two's are ticked off because they think they are number one. The number two's are leaving the company voluntarily. They are good employees, great hires, and they are very loyal. They don't speak up when they are dissatisfied because they consider it whining. They just say to themselves, "If they don't get it right this time I am out of here." I know, because I have been a number two before.

The dilemma becomes magnified in the learning curve years and less of a factor moving into golden years. What I mean here is that, as an employee moves to the eight-plus years of tenure with a company, things like stock options, retirement plan vesting, and four weeks of vacation become attractive reasons to stay put. But the two to five year veteran who has just completed their Masters degree can get a 50 to 60 percent increase by making a move. Compare that to the message they get in their annual performance review: "We think you are a number two performer, which is above average, so we will give you a 6 to 8 percent raise which is way above our average of 4 percent." If they are lucky they can get an additional equity adjustment or promotion to get it to a 10 percent increase. Compare that message, which happens annually (and will probably be the same next year, and the year after that) with the fact that the head hunters are calling weekly, if not daily, with promises of brighter horizons and the big bucks. It is difficult for them to say "not interested." And if they go on the interview, chances are they will get the job offer, because they are good (remember they are exceeding your expectations).

I am not suggesting that companies need to compete by giving number two's 50 percent raises, but we need to look for ways to send the right TRM message. The performance appraisal and annual merit review process is only the tip of the iceberg. It is time corporate America takes a hard look at the internal job posting and transfer process.

Internal Transfer Programs

The traditional job posting and internal transfer process has always been puzzling to me. I understand the politics, but the irony is just too much. Ever since automation has hit the HR function we have been devising ways to reduce the administrative burden so we can focus on more value added activity. Employee Self Service became the end all and some great applications, such as benefits enrollment, employee data update, and self nomination emerged. The self-nomination (a.k.a. job posting) programs are very necessary and provide employees with a great tool to take their career development into their own hands. Most HR professionals are familiar with the classic employee that will post for every job that has a word they can spell. The automated self nomination process helps reduce the burden of handling all of those job posting forms, acknowledgments to the employee, etc. You might also make the argument that by creating these slick automated tools for our employees, we have addressed the need for better promotional, transfer, and growth opportunities that we detected from our exit interview data.

Now that we are done patting ourselves on the back, let's take a closer look at what we are missing. The term Human Resources Management would imply that our jobs involve the management of the human resources (a.k.a. people) within the company. By relying on the self-nomination and/or job posting process to fill vacancies with internal resources, we are essentially taking our hands off the wheel and allowing the human resources to manage this process on their own.

To make it even worse, our archaic internal transfer policies are restrictive in nature. I know that many companies are making strides here, but, the typical internal transfer policy goes something like this:

1. You are eligible to post for a job if you have been in your current job for at least twelve months (with satisfactory performance, of course)
2. Your manager's approval is required if it has been less than twelve months
3. If you are eligible you need to complete the job posting form and get your manager's signature (as an acknowledgment, not approval), or, once you are in consideration for a position your manager will be notified
4. You may only post for up to two to three positions at one time
5. All jobs below a certain grade will be posted weekly and will remain open for seven days, we will also simultaneously advertise these positions externally (but for those seven days we give internal applicants preference). So be sure to look every week!

Think about the "un-TRM" message this sends to the employees. With all these restrictions, we make it easier for external candidates to get jobs than we do for our own, valued, employees who are known entities with known performance records. We spend huge budgets on advertising, recruiting software, Internet posting services, job fairs, and agency fees. We even tell our valued employees that we will give them a few extra bucks if they refer a friend. It gives credence to the old saying "I have to leave and come back if I want to get ahead in this company."

More importantly, how is this perceived by a number two employee. The number two employee is very loyal and feels awkward about getting a manager's signature on a job posting form. They work hard and do not take the time to job postings. So who is using the self-nomination program? While our valued number two's are leaving us, the number three and four employees are job posting machines. They post so often that statistically our self-nomination program looks like a huge success. Personally I don't mind when the number three employees get themselves a more interesting job by posting internally, but too often the job posting process becomes the mechanism for a manager to get rid of a number four. The manager may have been too chicken during performance review, so they often come disguised as a number three. This is why internal transfer, promotional, and growth opportunities are frequently rated as "poor" during an exit interview.

As we move our number three and four employees around the company, our number two's become frustrated and move on. We will never eliminate turnover, but the number two dilemma is a clear indication we may be turning over the wrong segment of the workforce.

So what's an HR function to do?

TRM Potential Solutions

As the labor market tightens, more and more companies are looking for more and more creative retention strategies. Rewards and recognition programs, casual day, retention bonuses, etc., are all fine strategies, but, I think we have a real opportunity as an HR profession to make a significant impact. It is time we take control and start managing those Human Resources.

Most large companies have invested in a major recruiting software package in the last ten years to handle résumé scanning, applicant tracking, and EEO reporting. For the most part these systems are used primarily (if not exclusively) for external recruiting (with the exception of the self nomination candidates).

Think about all of the résumés in your database as a talent community. As a recruiting function we have several options as to how we leverage that community. The most common approach is a Single Tiered Recruiting Model. This is somewhat of a reactive approach where we get a job requisition, we advertise, we post, and solicit more talent into the community. We then narrow it down to a select group that we will pre-screen, interview, and ultimately select a new employee. In the single tiered model much of the information that was collected in the pre-screening and interview process is not consistently stored in the recruiting system and therefore cannot be used to narrow down the talent community when the next job comes along. The Two-Tiered Recruiting Model is a more proactive approach where the recruiting function systematically reviews all of the talent that enters the community. The viewpoint here is that incoming résumés are nothing more than unqualified data (no matter how good your software is) that requires some human review to determine the value. In the process of the preliminary review of the data and the pre-screening additional information is systematically stored such as job classifications, salary requirements, geographic preference, availability, etc. This essentially divides the talent community into two tiers, unqualified data (those that have not yet been prescreened) and a pre-qualified talent pool (candidates for whom we know more information). In the two-tiered model, when a job requisition is received, the recruiter can instantly draw from the pre-qualified pool before tapping the unqualified data or soliciting more talent. This approach can save a great deal of time in the recruiting cycle and also reduce the costs. Many corporations are beginning to use this model, but, for the third party recruiting agency it is an absolute must.

Now it is time to take the next logical step and really leverage the investment in our recruiting technology with a Three-Tiered

Recruiting Model. The third tier of this model is the product of our hiring process, the employee base. Your employee population is the most valuable part of your talent community because you have such an extensive amount of information stored about them. You have performance rankings, career goals, compensation history, salary grade, length of service, gender and race, and just about any other piece of data you care to think about. By storing key portions of this information (in addition to a résumé) in your high powered recruiting database, when a job requisition is received the first step for a recruiter is to search the employee talent community.

With the three-tiered recruiting model, I can now seek out all of my number two (and/or number one) employees, currently one to two grades below (i.e. promotion opportunity), that would have interest in this job as career path, and meet the skill requirements of the job. I can even use the amount of time they have been in their current position as search criteria, if the politics are such that I still need to enforce that barrier. By adding gender and race to my search criteria, I can target females and minorities for requisitions that fall into an underutilized job category (imagine what this might do to the AAP results?!?). I can do all of this in a matter of minutes, before deciding to spend time tapping into my second tier, or spend money on building up the first tier. In addition to saving time and money, it sends a very positive message to the employees, telling them that you recognize and value their contribution and will reward them for their hard work. It tells them that you will truly pay for performance and that you prefer to promote from within (not just an HR slogan).

Most importantly, it gives me the power as an HR professional to help my company leverage and manage its most valuable asset, the human capital. It creates an opportunity to control retention in a way that will ensure we are turning over the right segment of the workforce.

Conclusion

Implementing a program like this is much easier said than done. There are corporate cultural issues, management styles, and politics that make this extremely challenging. It requires the evaluation of the effectiveness of the performance appraisal system and compensation programs including job classifications, salary grade structures, and ranking schemes. It requires a HR organization that can build credibility and trust with a line organization and truly shake the administrative, paper pushing, policing stereotype that HR functions often carry. Above all, it will require the commitment from the very top of the organization and a CEO willing to practice retention TRM at its fullest, i.e., stepping up to the retention challenge even if it means inflicting change upon the status quo.

CHAPTER FOUR

Employer-of-Choice Organizations

> "Leadership is the art of getting someone else to do something you want done because he wants to do it."

—Dwight D. Eisenhower

4

Leadership Strategies for TRM

JAC FITZ-ENZ PhD

Jac Fitz-enz PhD is the acknowledged father of human capital benchmarking and performance assessment. The Founder of Saratoga Institute, he carried out the original research on human capital measurement in the 1970s. Since then, the Institute has become known as "the source" for human performance and productivity data as well as for definitive research in HR. Dr. Fitz-enz has written seven books on value creation and human capital-related subjects. He holds a BA from Notre Dame University, a MA from California State University and PhD from USC. Dr. Fitz-enz can be reached at source@netgate.net.

It is clear to everyone that with the arrival of the millennium profound changes are sweeping the world. These are permeating all aspects of our lives from the most personal, to relationships with others, to our jobs, and to our nation. From a business standpoint, changes in the marketplace call for a review of our corporate vision and strategy. We have to recognize that managing and marketing our companies in the near future require our taking into account how customer and employee needs and wants are changing as both try to cope with the new world.

The hallmarks of the new market are several as noted in Figure 1. Along with changes in the market, organizational structures are changing. Sometimes these changes are not recognized until long after they have begun to reshape the organization without management's knowledge or leadership. The most pervasive forces reshaping organizational life are the worldwide web and intranet systems. The intranet does more than facilitate the collection and distribution of information. It changes the corporate communication channels and protocols. In effect, it flattens the organization more than any redrawing of the organization chart. It affects the culture of the company, whether or not management accepts it. When anyone can communicate almost instantaneously with

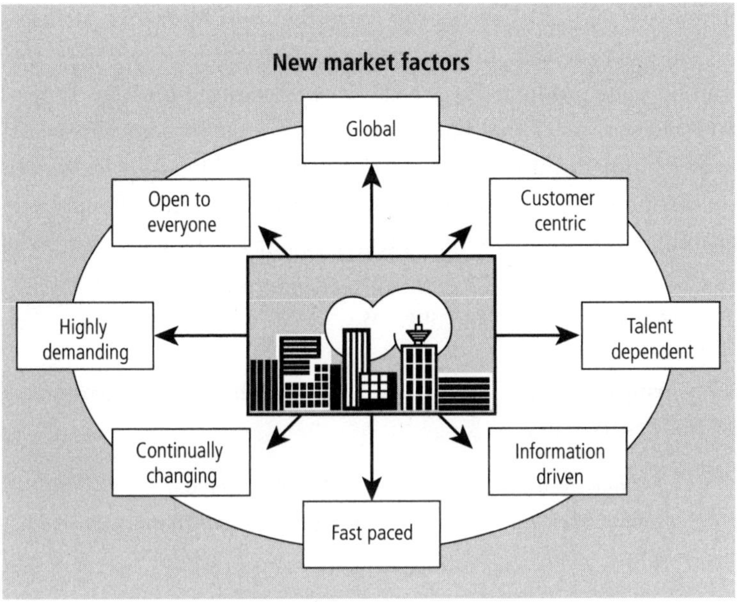

Figure 1. New market factors

anyone, anywhere in a worldwide organization that forms the base for a new culture. The collision of the new market and the new culture mandate a review of management practices.

Success Signs

Traditionally, business success was monitored through a set of financial and customer metrics. These included revenue, market share, earnings per share, customer retention, time to market, and product or service quality. In the new market all of the above still apply. However, the emerging organizational structures and cultures suggest new internal success indicators. Principal among these are three:

1. Effective leadership
2. Being an employer of choice
3. Managing talent relationships.

These are critical issues because even the most insensitive manager must accept that human talent and motivation are now the most potent productivity forces. In the beginning of the industrial revolution, capital plus manufacturing technology drove the growth and dominance of an organization. After World War II marketing spread the word and stimulated the desire of people to consume the products of industry. Today, for reasons that have been well publicized, people in the form of skills and knowledge are the primary drivers of success.

This brings us to the key question for the emerging organization of the 21st century:

How do we accelerate the capacity of our organization to compete on the basis of human capability and commitment?

Leadership

Leadership is still paramount for all the traditional reasons. But now it is even more critical because of the effect that it is having on market valuation of the corporation and on the retention of talent. According to researcher Leslie Gaines-Ross, the reputation of the CEO can account for as much as 45 percent of the company's market capitalization. The effects of top leadership changes have been profound in companies such as IBM, Coca-Cola, Motorola, and others. Internally our research has found that one of the key reasons people are choosing to leave their organization is lack of credibility on the part of their top executives.

The all-time number one topic in management literature is leadership. More has been written about it than about anything else. Theories abound. Pundits proclaim. Research is reported daily on leadership trends. Yet the question remains, Is leading different today than in the past? The answer is No. The characteristics of leaders have always been basically the same: vision, persuasion, and

According to researcher Leslie Gaines-Ross, the reputation of the CEO can account for as much as 45 percent of the company's market capitalization.

perseverance. What is different is the way in which leaders must become aware of themselves as messengers and resources for their people as the needs of their people change. Leaders aren't leaders until they have followers.

Two Sides

There are two sides to leadership: internal and external. The internal deals with the personality of the leader. Although a strongman can sustain his position and bull through any opposition for a period of time, the true test of a leader is the length of time he or she can capture and hold the allegiance of their stakeholders. The better leaders know themselves the better equipped they are to sustain the support of their Board of Directors, financial analysts, customers, and employees. Leaders who cannot retain the key talent of their organization have short tenures. Personal attributes that are critical to self-understanding are the person's sense of self —their identity, their character and trustworthiness, and their attitudes and beliefs about people—customers and employees. These factors will dictate the person's behavior and ultimately their long-term success as leaders or value creating companies.

The external aspects of leadership have to do with relationship skills, knowledge of the business, and savvy or know-how. There have been visionary leaders who could inspire the market and the employees with their perspective of the opportunities ahead. However, many of those people failed because they didn't understand their people and because they could not execute their vision. In the long term lack of knowledge and know-how dictate the odds against success.

Employer-of-Choice

So much as has been written about how a company can become an employer-of-choice that the term has come close to being an ill-defined cliché. The *Fortune* magazine lists of best companies to work for, research by pollsters, and position papers from consulting firms and research centers have accumulated more than enough information. The question is, how does one sort through all of that and find a few universal truths?

Our review of the accumulated literature has uncovered four predominant factors. These appear constantly in one form of expression or another in almost all reported research. The four factors are:

1. Humanitarian value system
2. Consistent executive behavior
3. Commitment of resources toward growth
4. Opportunity for people to learn and advance.

Humanitarianism

Ever since the publication of Douglas McGregor's seminal 1961 book describing Theory X (authoritarian) vs. Theory Y (humanitarian) styles of management, debate has raged over the most productive attitude for management to have regarding employees. By now the vast majority of managers have swung toward the side of Theory Y. Companies where this is the predominant style usually

Over reliance on expense reduction drives the company to the point of diminishing returns relatively quickly. It is an admission of lack of imagination or vision as to growth opportunities.

have performed better over time compared to those whose attitudes are more contentious.

Consistency is at least as important as humanitarianism. The worst offense a top executive or a line management can commit is inconsistency of behavior. It sets everyone on edge. People fear making decisions and performance wallows in mediocrity. Inconsistency is one of the reasons given by departing employees for their decision to quit. A bully that you know is at least better than a schizophrenic.

Commitment to growth is one of the most interesting phenomena we have observed throughout our career. Invariably when business slows down executives have to pull in the reins and slow growth until signs appear that the market is turning. Employers who prosper are those who see the turn more quickly and shift from expense reduction to revenue generation. Many turn around artists have made their reputation by selling off assets of sick companies. How much intelligence does it take to cut an organization to the bone and leave no muscle for future growth? Over reliance on expense reduction drives the company to the point of diminishing returns relatively quickly. It is an admission of lack of imagination or vision as to growth opportunities. Cutting cost is limiting, but revenue generation is stimulating.

One of the key differences that the 21st century workforce has over its 19th and 20th century predecessors is the need to take more from their job than a paycheck. While learning is a central human trait it is only within the past twenty years or less that many executives have come to accept that helping people learn and advance drives organizational growth and prosperity. Today, the success of the organization is tied to the success of the people inside it. Styles may be defined differently by industry or corporate culture but learning opportunity is clearly a hallmark of an employer of choice.

Talent Relationship Management

Workers today at all levels face challenges that their parents never knew. Executives who want to manage talent have to deal with at least a half-dozen forces. These include:

1. Shortage of qualified labor
2. A hyper speed world
3. Alienating technology
4. Weakened support systems
5. Need to constantly adapt
6. Demand for self-determination.

Qualified Labor. The GDP of the United States over the past forty years has outgrown the availability of qualified workers. As technology has been introduced into the workplace the population of educated technicians and professionals has lagged. There are not now, and for the next fifteen years there will not be, enough people capable of taking on the technical jobs that are becoming available.

Hyper Speed World. Electronic technology and high speed transportation have opened the world market to everyone everywhere. This has exploded the number of competitors that every business has. It is now possible for a small company on the opposite side of the globe to compete with any local producer of goods and services.

Alienating Technology. As technology has given us extended reach and increased speed it has separated us from our natural state. In many cases this is good as the crushing weight of physical labor has been greatly diminished for millions. Yet on the other hand as we are removed from our natural pace of life we experience separation anxiety without having a name for it. All we know is that in many ways our life is not as comforting as it was in "the good old days." This stress will continue.

Weakened Support Systems. Again technology gives and takes away. Just as it makes it possible for us to live long distances from our roots it also takes away the immediate support of the family and familiar community. The population explosion has rendered governments powerless to provide the support that many people need. Most institutions that were part of our bedrock cannot keep up with the changing world. People change faster than institutions.

Constant Adaptability. Speed again forces all of us to continually look for ways to meet the challenge of change. Laws, markets, competitors, and technology change so rapidly that everyone who wishes to keep up much less advance has to constantly learn and adapt to the changes. Twenty years ago as the one market world began to emerge we thought that we were moving from one world toward another. Now it is clear that this is the new world; the world of constant change and adaptation.

Self-determination. As we face the changes above we have two choices. One is to drop back and let the forces take over and dictate our lives for us. Millions upon millions do this particularly in impoverished areas where the weight of economic or political oppression is too great. However, in more affluent regions many people above the poverty level have risen up and proclaimed that they want a voice in how they will live. When they are denied that voice in their work place almost all of them choose to leave as soon as another opportunity appears.

Joiners, Stayers, and Leavers

The reasons people stay are different from the reasons people leave their employer. A recent major study found that age, seniority, sex and marital status have little bearing on staying with or leaving a company. The study did clearly identify the principal determinants of joining, staying, and leaving.

To begin, the favorable impression of the immediate supervisor is a strong determinant of someone joining a company. For salaried employees professional growth and advancement opportunity are influential. For hourly workers, work location and benefits are important. Yet for both, their impression of the immediate supervisor is key.

Summary findings of why people stay with a company are primarily compensation, recognition, and the behavior of their supervisor. For salaried employees technical growth and achievement recognition are important. For hourly people, compensation, growth, and good working conditions are essential to staying. Behind both though is still the immediate supervisor's behavior.

Finally, the principal reasons an employee leaves are frustrations with compensation, career growth, and supervisory behavior. For salaried personnel, lack of career direction and development are influential. For hourly workers, lack of compensation, growth, and poor management practices drive decisions to leave. But again, the power of the immediate supervisor is not to be ignored.

Conclusion

The lesson is clear. Long term success, success that transcends economic cycles, success that serves the community, success that fulfills employees is founded on irrevocable principles. These principles are consistency in leadership, humanitarian cultures, and systems that facilitate employee learning and growth.

> "The years teach much which the days never knew."

—Ralph Waldo Emerson, *Essays*

4

As Generation X-ers Enter the Workplace, HR Remains in the Hospital

ALFRED J. WALKER

Alfred J. Walker is a Senior Fellow with Towers Perrin. He is the Global Thought Leader and leading contributor of Human Resource Technology Strategy and Human Resource Effectiveness Practices. A well-known author, lecturer, and Summit Award winner, Mr. Walker's most recent textbook is titled *Web-based HR.* Adjunct professor at Rutgers University, Mr. Walker is a past president of IHRIM and founder of the New York Chapter of IHRIM. He holds a BS from Fordham University and MBA from Seton Hall. Mr. Walker can be reached at walkeaj@towers.com.

Bulletin: Future Workers Have Entered the Workplace

They are here, and they aren't happy. These new workers people are talking about, many of them born after 1965, are also labeled Generation "X-ers". They have been entering every workforce for sometime now, but they are a force in the Silicon Valley companies, Dot-Coms, and startups. Their presence places heavy demand for change on managers and co-workers. Gen-X workers are Internet savvy, live in a wireless world, and yet often have to exist in a workplace that operates twenty years behind the times. Their management has no clue how to deal with them, their corporation's IT functions often have no overall IT strategy, the customer relations and accounting processes are outdated and in many cases the company does not even have a standard e-mail system. They have the skills and abilities the business needs, they are highly technical and hard working, and they are the future workers of North America.

They also present a challenge to HR management and their function, since they want and need support from all four quadrants of the Total Rewards Attributes, (*See Figure 1*). In the past, most HR plans and programs concentrated solely on the bene-

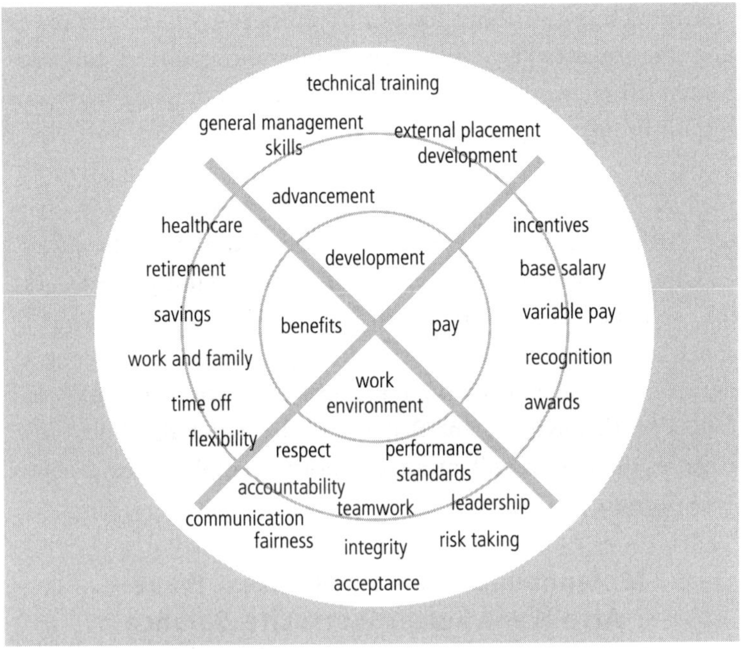

Figure 1. Total rewards attributes

fits and pay areas, since that was what traditionally motivated and retained employees.

But these new workers want more than just benefits and pay. And that is driving HR nuts, since most companies don't have well-defined programs in the work environment and development areas. The new workers are more mobile, feel little employer loyalty, and will readily job hop to get what they want—managers know it. Gen-X workers are not impressed with traditional organizations, authoritarian management styles, complex grading structures, or old-fashioned job titles. Unlike the generation before them, they are not interested in spending a lot of "time-in-grade" waiting for a promotion. In fact, many do not want to move "up" in the ranks at all, preferring learning and education in place of authority. They want to work on teams with a diverse set of people from other backgrounds and cultures. They care about the quality of their work and the products they make. They understand fully about CRM and customer satisfaction and they want to make a difference by working on important projects.

Gen-Xers also want a life outside the office, and strive for a better work-life balance. They have watched the "baby boomers" and the "greatest generation" sacrifice their family life for the job, and they don't want to give up that much. They want to spend more time at home with family, hopefully avoiding the 50 percent divorce rate of their parent's generation. If they can't find a work environment that offers them the flexibility they require, then they will move to another employer in a "New York minute."

Millennium Workers—The Next Wave—Also Want Better Work-Life Balance

The future worker issue is not just limited to the Gen-Xers. New research shows that the generation following them, labeled the Millennium Generation (although not yet felt in the workplace to any great degree) feels the same about work, or more so. Born after 1981, they are just entering college at this time. Studies of their preferences show an even greater desire than the Gen-Xers for harmony and responsibility. They are not as cynical or rebellious—their goal is to do the best thing they can for the family, the country, and the earth, and do it together, in a group. (Their interest in Buffy, Britney, 'N Sync, and the Gap ads, glorifies music, dancing, and fun in groups. This is more of an echo of the WWII Greatest Generation as opposed to the Boomer era where individuality was the trend.) The Millenniums also possess a strong need to do interesting and meaningful work, help others, and not worry about being "dot-com millionaires." They, like the Gen-Xers, put company loyalty far below fairness and finding a place where people appreciate them.

Future Workers Dissatisfied with Current HR Programs

Let's revisit the Total Rewards issue. Faced with these new workers, managers know they cannot attract, motivate, and retain them with outdated HR plans and programs that focus mostly on pay and benefits matters. It makes little sense to explain to them that they are entitled to a pension plan over which they have no investment control and will not receive any benefit until age 65. The Generation X workers want to have a say in when and how the money is invested, and further, they desire portability. These current plans, good in their time for a more stable workforce who often remained with the same employer up to retirement, deliver neither the control nor the portability that the newer worker wants. Similarly, the performance management and compensation plans that most companies offer do not satisfy the new workers. The traditional model is a base pay level tied to a grading structure, and perhaps bonuses that range from 5 to 20 percent of base for most salaried employees. Bonus amounts are generally clustered around the mean, and wide deviations from the market or position rate rarely occur. These plans offer little flexibility, so supervisors have difficulty producing any spread with a 5 percent budget cap. It's not a surprise that the newer workers see problems with this type of salary plan.

The issue starts in the performance management process in many companies. In the new technology-driven world, the ratings and payouts are controlled by the manager who may know what the employee has accomplished, but often does not, for a variety of reasons. It may be due to the multitude of projects that either the boss or subordinates are involved in, usually not with each other. Since many employees are individual contributors and work on geographically scattered work teams, direct work observation is often difficult, or the workers are simply not in the office. The popularity of telecommuting works against the performance evaluation process since the worker and boss may be seldom in the same place. Therefore, in this environment, it's folly to try to ascertain how the workers performed on targets and objectives set a year in advance and never adjusted. As a fallback, managers may use hearsay evidence or prior year's rankings. These methods are not very satisfactory in anyone's eyes.

Experience tells us that many managers also feel reluctant to radically differentiate performance in these situations since they will have to backup their decisions with factual citations about who is a better worker and why. Often they cannot do so. Add to this, that in the tight labor market even average performers get most of the job done, without much error, so managers are hesitant to come down hard on anyone for the sake of a percent or two difference in pay, or a few thousand dollars in bonus.

But, employees know who is producing and who isn't and want to see the right people get the largest raises. Problems occur when they find out that everyone receives about the same amount of pay increase regardless of efforts and results. Relying on stock options to make up the difference does not have the appeal they once did. Falling stock prices have put lots of options under water, and they may be under for some time. These plans fall well short of paying for performance, creating a no-win situation for all concerned.

Other HR programs need a major overhaul to fit these new employees as well. Career development plans in the past have led employees to focus on advancement in terms of traditional job titles in the larger departments such as finance, marketing, manufacturing, and information technology. With the fast-changing nature of businesses, the traditional areas are not where companies need help. There are more opportunities in places such as e-commerce initiatives, on task forces, in smaller organizations, and staff mergers and joint ventures. Some positions offer the chance of global assign-

What the newer worker wants is to put together their own "deal," covering pay and work rules. They do not buy into the rigid benefits and compensation plans, or the daily nine to five routine that has been traditional in the past.

ments. The HR function often is the last to know about these needs and as a result their systems are not supplied with the competencies and position requirements. Therefore, development programs and paths are not setup, and employees are not made aware of these opportunities, much less prepared or groomed for them.

Many newer workers want to work at home for part of their week. Some have childcare, or elder care issues. Others have life interests that demand a good bit of time away from the workplace. The structured work environment and commuting schedule offers little room for these activities. Since quality of life is a big issue for these workers, they will go where their demands are met. What the newer worker wants is to put together their own "deal," covering pay and work rules. They do not buy into the rigid benefits and compensation plans, or the daily nine to five routine that has been traditional in the past. They want flextime, interesting work; the ability to opt for newer assignments in growth areas and appreciation for their efforts. They care about customers and take along-term, compassionate view of their co-workers. So HR has its work cut out for them. They need to examine their plans and programs to see if they can meet the demands made by the new workforce, and update them if they fall short. They need to ensure that the organization and its management fully utilize the talents these workers bring (*See Figure 2*).

Group	What they want	Company's response
Greatest Generation	security, lifelong employment	retirement plans, seniority
Baby Boomers	advancement, wealth	titles, stocks, bonuses
Generation X	mobility, self-development	new employment "deal," lifelong learning
Millennials	achievement, working with people they like	diverse teams, projects, communitites of interests

Figure 2.

Medical Update: HR Still in the Hospital—Unable to Respond to the Challenge

We are now more than a year into the new century, and while we have already hired a good number of the new workers, we are sad to report that the "health" of the HR function has not improved substantially from what it was more than ten to fifteen years ago. Unfortunately, HR remains mired in its traditional role, delivering the same services in the same way. They have not updated their plans, but continue to offer old tired plans and programs that don't help managers manage or workers work. In numerous surveys, and in direct work with many companies, in all but a few best-in-class companies, it is apparent that most of the work performed in HR is predominantly administrative and routine in nature. It's not focused on helping the business with their most pressing people problems. Most companies have not transformed themselves in spite of the rhetoric over the last ten years that HR has now shifted to a more strategic mission and divested itself of the administrative activities that were holding it back. It is also in spite of the re-engineering efforts, massive expenditures on HRIS systems, outsourcing, and the somewhat futile attempts at HR transformation. Too much of the HR day is still spent on HR plan and program minutia, answering plan questions, paper pushing (yes, still), and record keeping tasks supposedly needed for regulatory compliance. To make matters worse, we are often told by managers, that the plans and programs are outdated, not connected with each other, don't work, and are not worth doing in the first place. They simply don't offer what the newer workers want.

And so, HR remains in the hospital. Although they may not be on life support or in the ICU, they are still in bed, not responding to treatment and unable to handle the challenges of the new decade.

HR'S Response

HR responds that they have attempted to change and institute new plans, but are working on more important issues like compliance, payroll, pension, and health and welfare programs. These matters cannot be handled by managers, whereas most of the aforementioned plans can. Therefore, it falls to the HR function to see them properly discharged. They contend that they have no choice but to work on these matters and this prevents them from assisting line managers with their business issues and administrative duties. They become resolved to a life of detail, assuring themselves that this work needs to be done, and done well. In the meantime, they give to the businesses what they can, when they can. They sense it is not enough, but they pride themselves on the fact that the shop is running and most of the troops are happy.

HR acknowledges that they have tried to change their focus over time, but most weren't able to divest themselves from the past and begin with new agenda. Many HR functions cannot procure the funds needed to cover both types of work. Unfortunately, many also feel that they may not have the skills and competencies to handle the interventions line managers want. Without the organizational consulting skills or the ability to devise a strategy, they may well feel trapped and unable to change their lot.

Management's Challenge to HR: Get Well and Fix It!

This should not be an either/or situation, but unfortunately HR has made it so. Enlightened senior management has little patience for this thinking and begun to challenge this notion of a downtrodden HR. Let's get on with it, management urges—we need you to help us. Almost a "If you can't get rid of the administration, I'll get rid of you" ultimatum. Get someone else to do the administration they say, or figure another way to get it done. Management recognizes that workforce problems are getting deeper, and HR's assistance in this will be critical in the future. Yes, we have new workers here who are not enthralled with the way we're organized and managed, so we really do need some help. The challenge—figure out how to change HR, or we will change it for you.

So What's the Prescription?

If HR functions really didn't matter, this wouldn't be a big deal. But it does matter. How to fix it? Management and HR must work together to create a new agenda for HR. They need to set new priorities and get on with the change issues, revamping the HR plans and transforming HR to shed itself of the administrative burdens and focus on the needs of the workers and management. As stated previously, there are new workers who need new plans, and the primary customers of HR (managers, both first-line supervisors as well as senior management) want and need HR's help. As an example, managers spend an inordinate amount of time on the recruitment process. Key jobs remain open for months and the corporation must often settle for what they rate as an average hire. They would love HR to add value to this process, perhaps by submitting a vetted short list for them to review, assisting with research on competitor or academic staffs that might be available or offering easy-to-use assessment tools.

And they should help streamline and shorten the overall hiring cycle—it is cumbersome and rife with approvals, turf issues, and wait times.

Additionally, HR could also be proactive in integrating the external hiring with the internal career development, transfer, and job posting systems. Is it any wonder that many HR plans don't work—within a single division of the company, or across divisions? Further, HR could devise better plans for filling jobs globally?

The hiring program is only one source of irritation that managers have with HR. Other programs that receive low marks include management development, succession planning, high-potential identification, performance management, organizational capability, knowledge management, and work-life balance plans.

Senior management must recognize that some necessary investments may stretch budgets for the next year or two, since an infusion of process work and technology to alter the work is needed. Similarly, an awareness of the value of outsourcing selected programs should be undertaken. Finally, a new set of competencies should be created to help place qualified HR staff in the individual business units to assist them with their people problems.

Is changing HR an important issue? Absolutely, if the company wants to grow and prosper in the future.

We have new workers here who are not enthralled with the way we're organized and managed, so we really do need some help.

Rx for Better HR Health

1. **Get up, get out of bed, and get out in the field.** Know your business and know your clients. Understand the demographics of your workforce and the underlying needs of the managers and employees.

2. **Develop some diagnostics.** Know how to assess the skills and abilities your workforce and HR staff needs to win in the marketplace and how to close any gaps. Ensure that your HR plans and programs are broad enough to meet the needs of all constituents.

3. **Take your medicine and transform the HR function.** Work on reducing the amount of administration, install new technologies, outsourcing any area that you cannot do expertly. Concentrate most of your HR resources on helping the businesses.

4. **Stay active.** Engage management and employees as necessary in the transformation and change process. Be sure to meet their needs as you go and communicate often on the progress being made.

5. **Install measurements that continually monitor HR's customer satisfaction levels and respond quickly to hot issues before they become major concerns.**

6. **Finally, move into rehab mode.** Stay flexible, open to change, and don't be defensive. HR plans and programs should not be cast in concrete. The workforce changes—plans should change to accommodate them.

This may not be the prescription you were hoping for, perhaps something quick and easy like taking two aspirin. The rehabilitation of HR is a more involved effort, but the rewards are great. You will bring value to the organization, help them be perceived as an employer of choice in the marketplace, and be in the forefront of organizational change. Act quickly, the Millenniums are coming.

> "Honesty is the first chapter in the book of wisdom."

—Thomas Jefferson

4

Getting Up from Down: How to Help Your Staff Live After Layoffs—and Help Downsizing Achieve the Results It Was Meant To

ROBERT J. McGARVEY

Robert J. McGarvey is a Tuscon-based journalist. He has written articles for magazines ranging from *Reader's Digest* to *Playboy*. He currently contributes regularly to *AmericanWay*, *Electronic Business,* and *Selling Power*. A particular focus of Mr. McGarvey's work: the psychology of business, and where the human element is recognized as a key factor in organizational performance. His website is www.mcgarvey.net. Mr. Garvey can be reached at rjm@mcgarvey.net.

Call it the downsizing one-two step. It's a predictable approach to the difficult problem of layoffs. First the CEO announces the bad news—the downsizing. That's one. Then, two, a quick shift into predictions of good times just around the bend.

There's just one problem: The vast majority of downsizing campaigns fail to meet their objectives. "Seventy-five percent of companies expect productivity gains, but only 25 percent achieve them," says management consultant Bob Turknett. Why? It's hard to eke more productivity out of demoralized and unhappy layoff survivors.

Huh? Isn't it enough for the remaining employees to have their jobs? Shouldn't that keep them happy? If ever there were a universal delusion among top executives, you just read it. Human resources experts are united in saying that post-downsizing, organizations have to take special steps to soothe and motivate employees, or watch employee morale tumble off the map. "Many organizations are so focused on the short-term boost to the bottom line that downsizing produces, they forget the potholes that await them down the road," says Nancy Kaylor, a workplace analyst.

Understand, none of this is academic. We're in the midst of a tidal wave of reductions in force expected to continue even as the economy improves. American industry sliced away almost two million jobs in 2001, according to Chicago outplacement firm Challenger, Gray & Christmas, and in early 2002 the pace continued. But despite all this practice, senior executives still fumble this mission because they aren't taking some basic steps, says Jim Mooney, Vice President of Consulting at Farr Associates in North Carolina.

Exactly what does a smart company do to handle the post-downsizing workforce? Follow the steps below, and you'll be on the right track.

Open Up

This is the essential starting point. The question on every mind is, Am I next? "The greatest failure of companies has been the lack of information," says Trey Graham, a Texas-based leadership expert. "Fear of the unknown haunts employees, so employers should comfort their workers by keeping them updated." Management may not fully know the future, but smart executives tell employees all they can to lower anxieties and get workers refocused on the tough rebuilding ahead. "Acknowledging and discussing workplace changes will go a long way toward preventing productivity paralysis," says Kaylor. "A little empathy never hurts."

Reorganize with Empathy

Do not heap "additional and unreasonable responsibilities on the remaining employees in a thoughtless way," advises Massachusetts career coach Gail McMeekin. That happens—lots—as managers try to parcel out all jobs among a thinner staff. "I've had clients say their bosses told them, 'You're lucky to have a job, so you have to do whatever we tell you,'" relates McMeekin. That is a sure way to push the best employees out the door. Won't some jobs go undone by a leaner workforce? You bet, so managers will have to be savvy about identifying tasks that can be delayed or ignored.

Recognize Survivor Guilt

In some cases, the survivors will believe more capable people were let go, and in other cases, they simply lost friends. Either way, the survivors need time for grieving. Acknowledge their losses, let them express their sorrow, and give them the space to vent. When management moves out of their way, they will probably get over this quickly—so encourage employees to express their emotions.

Ask for Input

Tap remaining employees for suggestions about putting the organization on a more prosperous path, says business management consultant Steve Koss: "It is amazing how few companies do this." A fast way to build team spirit—and to foster a sense that you're all in this together—is to solicit this employee feedback. Get employees talking, suggesting, thinking, and their optimism will be that much higher.

Conceive the Future

Kick up employee enthusiasm another notch with an exciting vision of the streamlined company. "They need to be shown that the new workplace will be better than the old," says Steven Rothberg, President and Founder of CollegeRecruiter.com, a jobs site that has had to downsize in leaner times. If employees believe that the downsized organization is just a skinnier, weaker version of what had gone before, he says, the very workers needed to create a new prosperity will seek new employment. Fight that, says Rothberg, by turning on employees to the new corporate direction.

Don't Stint on Back-Patting

"Demonstrate appreciation," says Kaylor. "In the post-downsizing weeks, look for opportunities to recognize teamwork, initiative, and commitment." Employees will be watching to see if their efforts are genuinely valued by management. Show that you care and—guess what?—employees probably will reciprocate by putting in the long, hard hours needed to propel the organization into renewed prosperity.

Job Survivor, Manage Yourself

Your organization has downsized, but your employer is doing nothing to help you cope with the new realities. That may be the everyday norm—too many companies still drop this ball—but smart employees are finding do-it-yourself cures. Such as:

- "Be very direct in questioning management about what is happening," says Marcia Reynolds, a Phoenix HR consultant. Knowledge may be the surest cure for downsizing's woes, so even when bosses duck the tough questions, keep asking, she says.

- You need to talk out your feelings—anxieties, guilt, depression—so when the employer doesn't provide a forum for venting, create your own, says Daphne Moses Houston, an employment counselor in Dallas. Talk with family and friends, and you'll also clue them into why you are moodier and more anxious than normal.

- New opportunities within the organization are probably open to you now, so grab them, urges Lin Grensing-Pophal, author of *The HR Book*. "Volunteer to take on responsibilities that no longer have a 'home,'" she says. Yes, these are sad times, but you still may wind up taking on responsibility that was out of reach before.

- Don't gossip, don't spread rumors, and stay positive, advises motivational speaker and author Patti Hathaway. It's easy to sink into negativity; don't. Stay upbeat. That's a key to positioning yourself for genuine success even amidst the challenges of a downsized workplace.

> "If there is anything that a man can do well, I say let him do it. Give him a chance."

—Abraham Lincoln

4

Employee Loyalty: It's Your Business

KEITH A. LAVINE

Keith A Lavine is the principal and founder of Morale Factory, a Chicago-based human resource consulting firm committed to guiding organizations in creating meaningful and engaging work and workplaces. His areas of expertise include employee motivation and job satisfaction, organizational assessment, management development, and employee selection. Mr. Lavine writes articles and speaks on employee motivation, retention, performance evaluation, and corporate consciousness. He received his MA in Industrial/Organizational Psychology from DePaul University. Mr. Lavine can be reached at keith.lavine@worldnet.att.net.

Today, it is hard to find an organization that is not scrambling to retain its employees, who are leaving in droves. It is a problem that is occurring everywhere, from large blue-chip corporations, to small boutique firms, to dot-coms. Even the public sector is affected. Recently, I was talking to a public school official concerned that even schools are losing too many excellent teachers and other staff to greener pastures.

Unfortunately, many, if not most organizations are reactive when it comes to retaining people. In other words, they tend to take action only after morale and turnover have become a problem. Likewise, managers typically don't know that a valued employee is dissatisfied until after that employee announces he/she is leaving.

Often, expensive counteroffers are made in a desperate attempt to change employees' minds. Assumptions are made as to causes of employee turnover (pay is usually, but falsely assumed to be the culprit). Recruitment and hiring efforts are stepped up in order to meet the organization's manpower needs. Financial incentives are increased throughout the organization in the hopes of building loyalty.

The problem is that these actions are seldom more than a quick fix to an organization's turnover issues (not to mention how costly the pay increases, as well as the continual recruitment efforts can be!) These actions treat the symptom of the problem, but do little to address the actual causes of the problem.

The fact is, many people today are looking for more from their jobs than financial remuneration and have an abundance of alternatives to choose from. They want and expect their jobs and the environments in which they work to be engaging. In other words, they want to be able to learn and grow, to feel intellectually challenged, to provide input and to make a difference. When people are engaged, not only are they more likely to stay with an organization, they are also more likely to:

- generate new ideas to increase revenues, cut costs, and drive growth
- deliver high quality service to internal and external customers
- brag about your organization to potential customers, employees, and investors.

Taking a proactive approach to employee retention requires a paradigm shift. Under the current paradigm, there is often an underlying belief that employees can't be trusted to be loyal and there is little an organization can do about it. As a result, a wait-and-see approach is taken. Only after an employee has demonstrated sustained loyalty is she fully recognized, rewarded, and valued.

Take for example a small advertising agency with which I've been talking. In an attempt to improve morale after a recent barrage of turnover, the owners of the agency decided to offer what they called a "bonus" to valued employees. Basically, they placed a sum of money into each employee's 401K plan. What would normally be construed as a magnanimous gesture on the part of the owners, has had little effect on job satisfaction, and may have even worsened morale for some employees. There are many reasons for

Just because an individual demonstrates he is able to successfully perform the functions of a job does not mean that he will be happy in his job and with the organization long-term.

this, one being the number of disheartening issues going on in the company that are not being addressed. Most importantly, the perception of employees to whom I've talked is that only employees who first reward the company by staying on board are valued and reap the benefits of the reward. Similarly, the message is that the owners don't trust people to stick around.

A proactive approach to retention means making a substantial investment in employees. It means taking the lead in building employee loyalty rather than waiting for employees to demonstrate loyalty before making an investment. This requires trusting that they will reciprocate when they are treated well. It means asking the question "How can we create an engaging environment for our employees so they'll want to stay?" as opposed to "What remedy can we come up with for our turnover problem?" Below are some specific and important actions that HR leaders and managers can take to proactively build employee loyalty.

- **Periodically assess employee morale.** More and more organizations are using surveys, focus groups, roundtables, etc., to understand how satisfied employees are with their work lives, and discover areas in which the organization can improve. This is an absolute must! It should be done on a regular basis to ensure the information is up-to-date. Where morale is low, turnover will be high. The mere act of asking for employee input can in and of itself improve morale. In addition, it will give the organization valuable information about key areas that need to be addressed in order for people to be engaged. Without a comprehensive assessment, management can only guess the key issues that need to be addressed. Of course, for there to be any benefit, actions must be taken to address these issues.

- **Select for fit, not just capability**. Many organizations have been revamping their hiring processes to ensure that they hire employees who have the knowledge, skills, and abilities to perform their job well. It is also important, however, to ensure that an applicant is a good all-around fit for both the job and the organization. It is really a person's overall fit that will best predict his long-term satisfaction and likelihood of staying and growing with an organization. Get to know the whole individual—their interests, values, aspirations, etc.—not just their capability of performing the job in the short-term. Just because an individual demonstrates he is able to successfully perform the functions of a job does not mean that he will be happy in his job and with the organization long-term.
- **Equip people to do their jobs.** This sounds simple, but employee training is often put at the bottom of the totem pole in terms of priority. Most people want to do a good job and contribute to their organization. There is nothing as frustrating as not being equipped to do so. I can't tell you how many managers I've worked with who never received even basic training on how to manage. Often, the technical training is there, but the training or coaching in people skills is lacking. It is the people skills that managers need in order to engage employees.

There is no question that training and development is a large expense, but so is employee turnover. The difference is that training and development has a return on investment; turnover does not. Remember that in order to retain valued employees, you need to invest in them and trust that there will be a payoff.

- **Find ways to engage individuals.** Every individual is different, and will be motivated by different things. There are certainly many programs that when implemented company-wide, should help engage large numbers of employees. Nevertheless, it is imperative for managers to get to know each of their employees and find out what engages them, or alternatively causes them to be disengaged. This information can help determine appropriate assignments for each individual, as well as communication styles, rewards, and goals that will be effective in motivating that person. Provide managers with coaching and/or facilitation in how to effectively engage members of their work group.

- **"Check-in" with individual employees.** As mentioned earlier, a mistake that many managers make is that they don't see signs of employee discontent until it is too late. Exit interviews can be a powerful tool to help understand why people leave and what changes need to be made. But isn't it even more powerful to "check-in" with each employee while he/she is still there? In addition to discussing projects, assignments, and performance, it is important for managers to periodically ask members of their work teams about their job satisfaction. Being closed off to this kind of feedback is dangerous. Being open to it is desirable. Actually soliciting this kind of feedback takes it one step further. Valuable information is gathered, and it also sends a message that the manager values the employee.

- **"Checking-in" can also be done on a formal basis.** More and more organizations are building an "upward feedback" process into their performance management systems, allowing employees to provide feedback to their managers. Another idea is to have a member of HR sit down with each employee on an annual or semi-annual basis to discuss job satisfaction, something usually only done during an exit interview.

Remember that in today's world, we are less likely to find lifetime employment contracts between employees and their employers. This trend began in the 1980s, with a slew of layoffs, and organizations demanding more for less from their employees. In a similar vein, employees are now demanding more from their employers. Greater efforts put forth by either party do not guarantee loyalty. However, organizations that are being proactive and taking actions to earn workforce loyalty are having greater success retaining their most valuable resource, their employees.

> "A weak man is just by accident. A strong but nonviolent man is unjust by accident."

—Mohandas K. Gandhi

4

Creating Organizational Justice: Where Talent Relationship Management Meets Employment Liability

JONI E. JOHNSTON PsyD

Joni E. Johnston PsyD is a clinical psychologist and the CEO of WorkRelationships Inc. She has been training organizations on workplace behavior training since 1982. Author of the best-selling *Complete Idiots Guide to Psychology* and brainchild of the popular and highly appraised *Appropriate Workplace Behavior* training series, Dr. Johnston has been instrumental in helping companies tackle workplace issues before they become costly court cases. Her firm has helped companies in Canada, the US, Finland, Mexico, and New Zealand reduce legal risks and increase profits through effective work relationships. Dr. Johnston can be reached at JJohns8780@aol.com.

Take it from someone who has heard more than her share of plaintiff's stories, employee complaints, and human resource nightmares. Create a climate of organizational justice and you'll make a significant dent in employee turnover, poor morale, workplace assaults, and employment liability. You'll have emotionally committed workers who are less stressed out and willing to go the extra mile. Yet, for some strange reason, organizational justice is one of the least understood—and underutilized—corporate weapons in the race to attract and retain top talent.

Of course, organizational justice is a complex concept that requires some serious work. It's certainly harder to implement than fancy perks, paid sabbaticals, or hefty bonuses. Yet, without a sense of perceived fairness, employees judge financial rewards less positively, and multiply the negative impact of challenging events (layoffs, difficult project deadlines, organizational chaos). In this article, we'll define organizational justice, clarify its relationship to employee productivity and employment liability, and offer strategies for creating a TRM climate that will help employers reap the rewards and reduce their risks of their human capital.

The Three Faces of Justice

On the surface, organizational justice seems to be a pretty simple concept; was a company or management decision fair? However, it's not just the outcome of a decision that matters; it's also how the decision was made and communicated. These three forms of organizational justice are known as distributive, procedural, and interactional justice.

Distributive justice refers to the "bottom line" of justice; i.e., was the outcome of a decision fair? These kinds of fairness issues often come up during pay raise decisions, layoffs, transfers, retraining, promotions, and demotions. They are also likely to arise in times of organizational change because new missions, policies, and procedures require changes in the structure of power and authority, and in the responsibilities and financial support of different programs.

Determinant of perceptions of distributional justice:

Comparison: Do employees perceive as fair what's happening to them when they compare it to what's happening to others?

Procedural justice focuses on how the decision is made; i.e., were the procedures used to set goals, make decisions, or investigate a grievance fair? While distributive justice focuses on the "ends," procedural justice on the "means." Questions of whether or not a procedure for allocating rewards is fair are equal to, if not more important, in decisions of distributive justice than any variables related to the size of the rewards allocated. In fact, even when workers don't like a particular outcome—being laid off, for example—studies show they exhibit less negative behavior when they perceive their layoffs as fairly decided.

Determinants of perceptions of procedural justice:

Consistency: Are the procedures applied consistently across time and other people?

Bias suppression: Are the procedures applied by a neutral person who has no vested interest in the outcome?

Information accuracy: Are the procedures based on information that is perceived to be true?

Correctability: Does the procedure have built-in safeguards that allow the employee to appeal?

Representativeness: Was the procedure designed based on the input of all affected parties (coworkers, customers, management, etc.)?

Ethicality: Are the procedures consistent with prevailing moral standards?

Interactional justice pertains to the behavior of the organization's leaders in carrying out their decisions; i.e., how they treat those who are subject to their authority, decisions, and actions. Do supervisors allow workers to have a voice in decision-making? Do they adequately communicate the ground rules of change? Research shows that the effects of interactional justice are independent of individuals' evaluations of fairness regarding the outcomes they receive (i.e., distributive justice) or the procedures used in allocating those outcomes (i.e., procedural justice) and, in some contexts, may be more important.

Determinants of perceptions of interactional justice:

Explanation: emphasize aspects of procedural fairness that justify the decision

Social sensitivity: treat the employee with dignity and respect

Consideration: listen to the person's concerns

Empathy: identify with the person's feelings

Interactional Justice: TRM Up Close and Personal

Interactional justice is a key to areas of talent relationship management devoted to employee motivation, employee retention, and organizational commitment. In a survey of 225 employees at two large US paint manufacturing companies, researchers found justice consistently trumped job satisfaction in motivating employees. However, it wasn't interactional justice in general that was the key; it was the employee's faith in their supervisor and the fairness implicit in day-to-day transactions.

Employees view the organization through their supervisor. It is mostly the supervisor that explains the organization to the employee and explains the employee to the organization. Not surprisingly, then, it is the personal assessment of a supervisor's honesty, impartiality, and integrity that causes employees to go the extra mile past where they had to go to get their jobs done. In its simplest terms it is the answer to the question: Can I count on this person's integrity?

Leaders seen as fair command more trust, respect, and commitment. In one study, supervisors who were regarded as fair or unfair in situations where they recommended higher or lower pay, based on merit, for work performed. Unfair supervisors commanded little commitment, even from higher-paid workers. Fair supervisors, on the other hand, commanded much more commitment—even from those who were paid lower. In addition, workers chose to remain with a supervisor who enacted procedurally fair behavior and they chose to leave the supervisor who did not—regardless of the supervisor's assessment of their performance and the pay outcome associated with it.

A recent Gallup study of two million employees at 700 companies revealed that most workers rate having a caring boss higher than money or fringe benefits. The study, reported in the *New York*

Times, also found that employees' productivity and their length of stay at their companies were determined by their relationship with their immediate supervisor.

Teaching Interactional Fairness to Managers: Interpersonal Skills + Leadership

Supervisors with transformational leadership style are better able to influence employees to perform extra duties by creating more procedural justice and trust. Researchers think this is because transformational leaders are able to inspire and appeal to their employee's sense of fairness and trust, which results in creating positive social exchanges between the employee and his organization. Their followers are compelled to work harder and conscientiously, making suggestions, performing extra duties, and helping others.

Such leadership styles are characterized by:

Clarification of responsibilities and expectations

Explanation of tasks that must be performed and benefits to self-interest

A contingent reward system

Followers have a positively reinforcing relationship with the leader

The leader only intervenes when things go wrong

A lack of personalization of the working relationship

In addition to a transactional leadership style, employees judge their manger's sense of fairness on the following interpersonal skills:

Consistency—the extent to which a subject treats staff consistently and does not play favorites

Decision-making—the extent to which a subject is unbiased and impartial in making decisions

Empathy—the extent to which a subject can see things from the perspective of his or her staff

Equality—the extent to which a manager treats employees like equals rather than as inferiors

Relative fairness—how fair the manager is relative to other managers within his or her organization

Supportiveness—the extent to which a manager provides substantive, symbolic, and emotional support to employees

Transactional fairness—the extent to which a manager is fair and non-exploitative in resource exchanges with employees

Treatment—the extent to which a manager is respectful and sensitive in interactions with staff

Voice—the extent to which a manager is open to the advice and feedback of staff.

Organizations who hire or promote managers and supervisors strictly for their technical skills, or who fail to provide an interpersonally oriented management development program as part of the promotion process, are missing a critical TRM opportunity to simultaneously increase employee retention and management effectiveness.

Serving Justice During Offensive Behavior Complaints

Most lawsuits are the result of misunderstandings, not malice. The remedy sought—money damages—is a poor but often emotionally necessary substitute for the employer's timely expression of empathy and validation of a plaintiff's hurt. This is especially true of claims arising in the employment context. Sexual harassment, discrimination, and wrongful termination claims, being interpersonal in nature, can often be solved in a personal way.

The most effective way to avoid crippling claims is to implement early, effective intervention through comprehensive management training focusing on the establishment of fair, consistent, responsive policies. This prevents management from losing their objectivity or effectiveness when confronted with emotionally complex problems or being embarrassed to the point of inaction. Simple misunderstandings can then be promptly and thoroughly investigated and dealt with immediately and suitably. The claimant should be assured that the claim is being taken seriously and should be kept informed as to the progress of the investigation.

The most effective way to avoid crippling claims is to implement early, effective intervention through comprehensive management training focusing on the establishment of fair, consistent, responsive policies.

On the other hand, treating each complainant as a potential plaintiff increases the risk that the civil claim will escalate. There are often two layers of hurt, disappointment, and betrayal involved with employment claims. In an effort to build team spirit and company loyalty, employers not infrequently use the "loyal family" or "team" analogy. Consequently, an aggrieved employee expects the "head" of the family or team to respond decisively and supportively. Too often, though, the opposite occurs: The employer isolates the charging party, fails to aggressively and objectively investigate the allegations, and fails to keep the charging party informed, thus (in the claimant's eyes) inflicting a secondary injury that can be more painful than the primary injury. Empathetically acknowledging the employee's underlying hurt does not constitute an admission of either liability or intentionally.

Sometimes a manager lacks the management skills necessary to deal effectively with a potential powder keg involving a subordinate. Managers must be encouraged to seek assistance when such a situation arises, so that, if necessary, it can promptly be identified as a crisis and an outside crisis manager brought in. In a crisis, chain of command thinking, "papering the file," and career worries cannot be permitted to interfere with effective solutions.

Believe me, fairness is something jurors relate to. In fact, jurors sometimes unconsciously shift the burden of proof to the employer to justify an offensive behavior investigation that fails the "smell test," i.e., when the jury doesn't approve of the manner in which the claim was handled.

The Straw that Breaks the Camel's Back: Workplace Violence, Theft, and Other Forms of Revenge

Failing to provide critical information on a project. Spreading malicious rumors about co-workers. Destroying or stealing company equipment. Giving classified product information to a competitor. These are just a few of the ways I've seen employees retaliate toward a company for perceived injustices. Plaintiffs don't talk about distributive justice (I'm suing because I lost my job or because I was sexually harassed) nearly as much as they relate stories of interpersonal inconsideration and abuse (no one took my complaint seriously, I was marched out the door accompanied by a security guard).

In a work environment, revenge occurs in response to violations of trust; i.e., when expectations concerned another person's behavior are not met, or when that person does not act consistent with one's values. Violations of interpersonal justice tend to evoke the strongest emotional responses, ranging from anger to moral outrage. There is evidence, for example, that dismissals or terminations do not provoke violence in and of themselves. Rather, vengeful attitudes and behaviors result from the humiliation that occurs when terminations are conducted in an abusive and insensitive manner. In fact, numerous studies have found a relationship between distributive justice (being terminated, for example) and retaliation only when there was low interactional and procedural justice.

Over 80 percent of the cases of workplace homicide involve employees who want to get even for what they perceived as their organizations' unfair or unjust treatment of them. This is not to deny the role of individual differences and how they interact with different workplace situations. An employee who explodes may have a higher level of aggression to contribute to the outburst.

In addition, various conditions in the workplace play a role in heating up tempers at work. Downsizings, layoffs, cutbacks in wages and benefits, and outsourcing all increase pressure at work; however, layoffs, disciplinary actions, or dismissals do not provoke violence by themselves; it is the wounded pride and loss of face that occurs when actions are conducted in a demeaning manner. It's the interaction between distributive, procedural, and interactional justice that leads to retaliation; unfair or unjust treatment during the termination interview may be the "last straw" or the final "push" that moves the terminated employee from retaliatory thoughts to actual retaliation.

Retaliation at work doesn't just occur in response to interpersonal abuse or humiliation; it can also result from the perceived violation of a psychological contract; i.e., beliefs in paid-for-promises or reciprocal obligations. For example, unrealistic sales projections to a candidate during a hiring interview, for instance, can lead to a sense of betrayal and injustice. Violation of the psychological contract is a process that contains elements of unfulfilled promises that deprive employees of desired outcomes (distributive justice) and elements that affect the quality of treatment employee's experience (procedural justice).

Unfortunately, this happens all too often. In a study of 128 MBA students, who had already accepted an offer of employment, 54.8 percent of the subjects reported that their employer had violated their psychological contract. This violation was significantly related to low scores on a measure of the employee's trust in his or her employer and to low scores on a measure of employee satisfaction. The results also suggested that employees who left the company reported a greater degree of contract violation than those who had not left their employer. Apparently, these violations spanned all areas of employment (e.g., training, compensation, promotion, nature of job, job security, feedback, management of change, responsibility).

Improve Your Fairness Quotient to Become An Employer-of-Choice

Any organization that wishes to excel must make sure that the employee-employer relationship is cast outside the economic relationship into the emotional arena. Human resources can play a vital role in organizational justice by monitoring the fairness of employment policies and procedures and ensuring that supervisors are inspiring employees toward goals. The following steps are in order:

1. Check all policies and work rules to assure that there are procedures that create fairness. The important ones center on pay, diversity, etc. Look at decisions made in implementing these rules and general working practices to assure that fairness and equality is explicit in all supervisory and management decisions about employees and their work. Don't forget the management employees.

2. Include leadership and interpersonal skills in your management development program, including 360-degree evaluations by subordinates, co-workers, and management. Include aspects of distributive, procedural, and interpersonal justice into job descriptions and make them part of the performance review process.

3. To guard against unintentional psychological contract violations, make sure all candidates are provided with "realistic job previews" (i.e., providing an accurate description of the job, organization, and opportunities, including both positive and negative features). The degree of honesty shown for employees during the selection process will shape perceptions of support and justice among those who are ultimately hired.

4. Because employees are most likely to engage in revenge either to restore equity or express feelings of outrage, provide multiple avenues for employees to deal with grievances (and the feelings associated with them). For example, in addition to formal grievance procedures, engage your EAP to give informal talks during corporate transitions and offer outplacement services during layoffs.

5. Teach your managers AND employees how to handle sensitive situations. For example, make sure your managers understand the "psychology" as well as the legalities of offensive behavior and termination. Don't exclude your employees from your harassment/discrimination prevention training; lower level employees are much more likely to be involved in employment lawsuits, yet they receive the least amount of training.

6. Train and monitor your supervisors' performance management skills. When employees evaluate the fairness of their performance appraisal, they focus on whether or not the appraisal process is consistent across employees, accurate, free from supervisor bias, allows for appeal if there is a disagreement, involves all parties, and is adequately justified.

The Bottom Line

Columbian author Gabriel Garcia Marquex once said, "Justice limps along . . . but it gets there all the same." Organizations who create a sense of organizational justice will reap the human capital rewards in improved motivation, retention, and fewer employment lawsuits. Unfortunately, companies who don't may find themselves limping while their competition runs ahead.

> "The genius of a good leader is to leave behind him a situation which common sense, without the grace of genius, can deal with successfully."

—Walter Lippmann

4

Managing the Resource Pool: The Right and the Wrong Way to Manage Human Capital

GARY A. BOLLES

Gary A. Bolles is an independent consultant specializing in strategy development and execution for early-stage companies, especially software and media. A frequent lecturer and speaker, he is also a contributing editor to *CIO Insight* magazine. Mr. Bolles has been on the startup management team of several successful software startups, including serving as the founding Chief Operating Officer for Evolve Software; as the Vice President of Marketing for Network Products Corporation; and led the founding of Ziff Davis Internet, the on-line arm of the technology media company. He is the co-founder and contributing editor of *Conferenza* (www.conferenza.com), the premier site for hi-tech events. Mr. Bolles can be reached at editor@gbolles.com.

An organization's workforce is really an aggregation of problem-solvers. Using tools such as information, technology, and each other, workers apply their knowledge and skills to solve problems for their employers. Problem is, employers too often fall into the mindset that only they know how to best allocate these human resources, and increasingly using software such as human capital management applications to do it. But if they don't approach the process with the right mentality, they'll end up wasting the talents they've hired.

Look at the vast range of moment-by-moment problems that each individual inside an organization solves in a given day. Suppose an average of 100 people solve an average of 100 problems. That organization could be said to have a daily ledger of 10,000 organization-wide problems needing to be overcome. Now suppose there's a hierarchy of these problems. Some are devilishly complex; others, insultingly simple. Give each problem a "difficulty value", ranging from one (easy) to ten (hard), with an average of (you guessed it) five. So let's say that, after an inordinate amount of time and a mountain of cash spent on consultants, you determine that the aggregate mountain the organization has to climb each day is 50,000 "problem units". Now, look at the organization's entire mass of people-power, including full-time and part-time employees, as well as consultants, contractors, and outsourcing companies. Suppose you can precisely quantify their skill levels at solving the problem-units they face each day, skills that exactly match the difficulty level of the problem-units those individuals face. In an apples-to-apples world (which, of course, only exists in our minds), multiplying their skill levels times the problems they face would equal 50,000 problem-units correctly solved. The result: An organization with "balanced" human capital, with human resources exactly meeting the needs of its organization-wide problems. That's great for today. What about tomorrow? Suppose the organization is growing rapidly, and the number of problems doubles in a year. Suppose the difficulty level of the problems also doubles in a year. Soon you'll have 200,000 problem-units to solve. How are those people—who can only solve 50,000 problem-units today—going to deal with this?

You could work everybody harder. Longer hours = more problems solved. But that's not especially cost-effective in many industries, over the long haul. (And in France, the trend has gone exactly the opposite direction, with the newly-mandated shorter work-week. Are we in the wrong country, or what?) You could set the bar higher, cutting loose everyone you deem ineffective, and hiring only people you think can solve the most difficult problems. More expensive in the long run, though, because only the most senior people could be hired in any job.

You could assess the work people do, making it more efficient. The fewer number of problems to be solved, the more people can solve in a day. (Weren't efficiency experts outlawed in the 50s?)

You could hire a lot of people really, really fast. (Welcome to the

You must continually put in place processes that focus on and enhance the individual worker's right to make their own decisions.

dot-com boom.) You could outsource even more. Expensive, too.

You could train the people that you have to better meet the challenges of tomorrow.

And so on. In fact, most organizations do all of these things, to varying degrees, at different times. But, of course, human capital management never really works in such a straightforward manner. It's messy and inefficient. Exactly the right skills are rarely effectively applied to exactly the right problems. And it's impossible to predict exactly what kinds of skills you'll need tomorrow. But that doesn't mean these challenges can't be addressed; it just means you have to accept the ambiguities inherent in resolving them. The truth is, both sides of the equation—organizational need and human capability—are extraordinarily flexible, and each can be adapted to the other based if need be.

The biggest challenge for organizations is to avoid taking this "pool of resources" mentality too far. Despite its title, human capital management can dehumanize the process of finding, hiring, training, and allocating the talents of people. How can you avoid this? There's a simple requirement, complex in the performance: You must continually put in place processes that focus on and enhance the individual worker's right to make their own decisions. There's a growing body of knowledge that shows that networked systems—and what company isn't a network of human resources?—gain value exponentially when they're self-organizing. That doesn't mean you have to promote anarchy. But it does mean that putting the power of deciding where to focus their talents in the hands of employees is absolutely the most effective way to encourage the greatest possible contribution by the people in your organization.

> "The world does not pay for what a person knows. But it pays for a what a person does with what he knows."

—Laurence Lee

4

Why Top Talent Looks Elsewhere

JOHN BOUDREAU PHD   WENDY R. BOSWELL PHD

BENJAMIN DUNFORD   PAUL R. RAY, JR.

John Boudreau PhD is a professor at Cornell University and Director of its Center for Advanced Human Resource Studies (CAHRS). He is recognized worldwide for his breakthrough research on the bridge between superior human capital and sustainable competitive advantage. He can be reached at jwb6@cornell.edu. Wendy R. Boswell PhD is assistant professor at Texas A&M University. She teaches and does research in HR management particularly around employee attraction and retention. She can be reached at wboswell@tamu.edu. Benjamin Dunford is a PhD student at Cornell University. He can be reached at bd33@cornell.edu. Paul R. Ray, Jr. is Chairman and CEO of Ray & Berndtson, the world's sixth largest executive search firm. He can be reached at pray@swbell.net.

Top executives don't look for new positions because they need the money. Abstract factors such as an ability to take pride in their work, interesting and challenging work, responsibility, and variety are typically critical considerations when an executive weighs a decision to change positions. Consider which factors the 1,607 executives who responded to the Ray & Berndtson/Cornell study ranked as important in considering a new opportunity:

A Study by Ray & Berndtson and The Center for Advanced Human Resource Studies—Cornell University

Intangible work characteristics	% of respondents who indicated "very important" or "important"
Pride in your work	97
Interesting work	95
Challenging work	95
Responsibility	91
A job well done regardless of rewards or recognition	89
Variety of experiences	86
Professional growth	81

Working hard	78
Autonomy	78
High pay	75
Discretion	70
Rewards	69
Ability to build a professional reputation	67
Recognition or praise at work	61
Promotions	50
Recognition from others in the field	47

The View from Ray and Berndtson

Executives want to build something—not merely maintain a program or product that someone else has launched. They seek a challenge where they can demonstrate their talent, not a maintenance role. They want to be connected to the top of the company, play a key role, and make a difference to the organization—at a nearly age. And they want to be recognized, paid, and promoted on the basis of their performance—not political savvy or seniority. Independence, responsibility, growth, and variety of experience are essential to top performers, whether in big or small companies.

It's difficult to predict how a candidate's attitudes about compensation and intangible factors will determine his or her reaction to a specific position. However, companies can enhance their attractiveness to top talent by communicating the symbolic and intangible aspects of the opportunities.

Most executives also value compensation highly for symbolic reasons. In Corporate America, it reflects status, rank, and achievement and validates long years of effort. When this important symbol falls below their expectations, executives are more likely to search for new positions, no matter how happy they are with their current situation.

Stock options—the right to purchase company stock at a below market price—became an important symbol of success during the 1990s and have gained widespread popularity for attracting and retaining management talent. Stock options also represent an opportunity to cash in on a company's success and expand an executive's net worth exponentially. Options motivate executives to build the long-term value of their company's stock.

The Ray & Berndtson/Cornell survey is the first to comprehensively measure the impact of a key compensation element —stock options—on job search activities. Our research found that the greater the proportion of options that are "underwater", that is with a strike price above the current stock price, the more frequently executives call recruiters, reconnect with their networks, prepare or revise their resumes, talk to prospective employers, and conduct other job search activities.

Companies committed to retaining talent should:

- **Make intangibles tangible:**
  Use recognition and rewards to make pride, interest, challenge, responsibility, and variety as fundamental to execute position descriptions, expectations, and revenue increases, profits, and market share.
- **Monitor market price relative to option strike price:**
  The point at which the market price of the stock drops below the strike price is a key psychological reference point that prompts executives to begin searching for a new position.
- **Recognize the opportunity cost of underwater stock options:**
  Executives who remain with their current organization can view underwater stock options as a downside risk when competitors begin offering penalty-reducing "option buyouts."

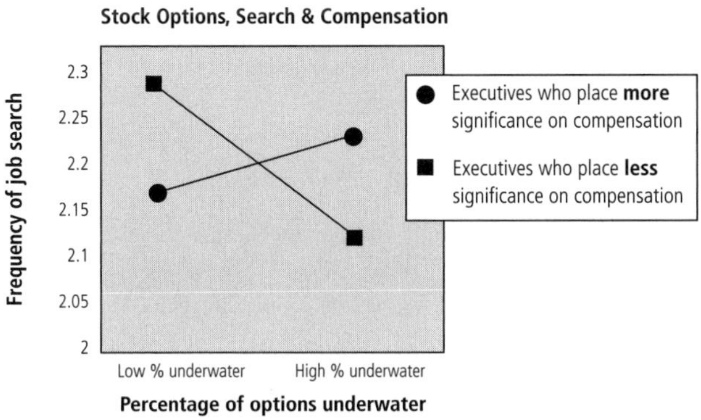

Executives who place greater significance on compensation (as a symbol of hard work, success, or achievement) search *more* when more of their options are underwater. Those who place less significance on compensation search *less* when more of their options are underwater.

Study method
Questionnaires were mailed in August 2000 to a sample of executives selected from Paul Ray Berndtson's database. Respondents completed 218 written questions about their current positions, job search activity, career, compensation, and attitudes toward work and money. There were 1,607 respondents, of which 856, or 53.3% owned stock in their current company, and 846, or 52.6% held stock options.

Respondent profile
Respondents, who averaged age 39 were senior executives representing a variety of companies and industries throughout the US. The typical respondent, who averaged age 39, holds an executive position 1.9 levels below the CEO at a public company more than $2.51 billion in annual revenues. He has worked there for an average of 5.5 years and has been in his current position for 3 years.

Compensation profile
The average respondents annual compensation, including base salary and bonus, is approximately $295,344, of which around 17.5 percent is payable in stock options. The typical respondent has already built up a significant nest egg, with average net worth of $2,324,864.

CHAPTER FIVE

Managing TRM Automation for Workplace Effectiveness

> "The talent of success is nothing more than doing what you can do well; and doing well whatever you can do. . ."

—Henry Wadsworth Longfellow

5

The Devil Is in the Details

WILLIAM M. KUTIK

William M. Kutik is considered the leading independent analyst of the HR technology marketplace with a special emphasis on Electronic Recruiting. A technology columnist for *Human Resource Executive* for over a decade, Mr. Kutik has also served as Co-Chairman of the magazine's annual trade show, HR Technology Conference & Exhibition, since it started in 1998. For seventeen years, he has been consulting editor for Esther Dyson's leading computer industry newsletter, *Release 1.0*. Previously he was the founding editor of the monthly magazine, *Computers in HR Management*; managing editor of Ziff-Davis' *Computer Industry Daily*; and a reporter for *The New York Times* and *The New York Daily News*. A Harvard University graduate, Mr. Kutik is President of Kutik Communications, a strategy and marketing consulting firm in Westport, CT. Mr. Kutik can be reached at bill@kutik.com

The Devil Is in the Details

The résumé has bedeviled every attempt to automate recruiting since the first packaged Applicant Tracking Systems appeared in the early 1980s. A succession of technologies have been used to impose (or extract) structure on the résumé—perhaps the most idiosyncratically structured (but persistent) of all standard information documents.

Since the résumé does not seem to be going away, a brief history of how we've tried to structure and search through them is important. Even today, the volume of résumés created by the Internet—and the information access problems they create—are a formidable barrier to recruiters actually practicing Talent Relationship Management.

Now a new breed of intelligent searching and matching engines based on various high-level programming techniques once lumped together as "Artificial Intelligence" hold out the promise of a new solution.

The Earliest Solutions

It all started with file folders of active paper résumés on a recruiter's desk. Since each one was written and formatted somewhat differently (name, address, and phone number at the top was about the only certainty), the first technology recruiters used to create a common structure among them was the yellow highlighter, still in use today! After a candidate was hired, the other résumés were put away in boxes and stored in a back room for three years to meet EEO requirements.

The earliest computerized Applicant Tracking Systems (ATS) were designed to replace both the file folders and the boxes. They were simple computer databases set up with correct fields and records to categorize applicants (by job codes, skills, education, etc.); keep track of them as they moved through a company's hiring system; and generate appropriate correspondence.

One of the earliest packages was an add-on module to the MSA (Management Science America) mainframe HRIS. MSA later became part of Dun & Bradstreet Software, now GEAC. The first PC package called ResTrac came out in 1982 from a company then called MicroTrac Systems (later Restrac) and now doing business as Webhire.

In addition to simple tracking, those systems for the first time gave users the ability to search through previous applicants to fill current open requisitions and do skills matching. This was a first because those back room boxes usually had the paper résumés from older requisitions stored alphabetically or chronologically, rather than by skill or job category, making any effective searching almost impossible.

But the early ATS did not replace the yellow highlighter! Recruiters still had to highlight and code each résumé, handing it off to a data entry clerk to enter the name, address, phone number, date received, and skills and experience into the system for future access. Even in the 1980s, the number of résumés received made the data entry challenge so daunting that few résumés were entered into the system, meaning the ATS was rarely useful for retrieval and skills matching, just tracking.

Enter résumé scanning.

The Rise of Résumé Scanning

Back in 1989, two companies on different coasts—Resumix in Silicon Valley and Restrac outside Boston—set about convincing HR departments that the automated entry of the full text of applicants' résumés using optical scanners was the next great idea. At the time, their founders saw them mostly as automated data-entry devices for an Applicant Tracking System, which could finally be used to its full potential.

In addition to storing the full text of résumés, both recreated (but automated) the existing system of recruiters structuring the résumé by highlighting it and clerks entering the pertinent data.

Today, most résumé processing systems fundamentally work the same way those first ones did thirteen years ago. Critical information (name, address, experience, education, etc.) was parsed or identified by software, extracted to fill the appropriate fields in the database record, and then checked by a person. The processing offered so many opportunities for errors (inaccurate optical character recognition, faulty parsing) that a human being always had to be involved to check the fields against the original résumé—what the industry has long called "stare and compare."

The resulting database records were then searched by those fields or by keywords against the stored full text of résumés to find a match for an open position (more on matching below). Resumix worked a little differently. After extracting the relevant information, it automatically assigned the applicant to a job category already built into the system. The full text of the résumé was rarely searched. But the problem with that technique was maintenance: The system required creating new detailed job categories as the variety of candidates expanded. In the software world, that is known as "pre-written logic," and it is expensive to maintain.

No one was ever delighted by either result. But there were other benefits, noted even back in 1990, by a short-lived magazine "Computers in HR Management" which wrote:

"While it's not perfectly clear that résumé scanning will save either time or money except in the highest volume situations, the systems definitely improve the quality of the applicant pool by making everyone in it accessible to recruiters in ways manual and traditional computer systems simply cannot match. . . .These systems will definitely give you better information to support faster hiring of better employees. In this day of a shrinking labor supply, just what is that worth?"

Sound familiar?

The basic process Restrac and Resumix created to deal with résumés in the late 1980s was re-engineered by iSearch and HireSystems (now BrassRing) in the 1990s.

The New Challenges

The basic process Restrac and Resumix created to deal with résumés in the late 1980s was re-engineered by iSearch and HireSystems (now BrassRing) in the 1990s. iSearch (now defunct) created a centralized factory to do the parsing and extraction work on an outsourced basis; BrassRing used the Internet to create a distributed factory of homeworkers for the same purpose.

Resumix and Restrac remained the leading systems well into the 1990s, when the Internet created a new challenge to recruiters. The rise of job boards and their huge résumé pools deluged recruiters with thousands of unqualified applicants for every job posted on a board or every search run against those pools.

After sourcing on the Internet, recruiters now often face a virtual pile of 5,000 résumés for every requisition with no easy or inexpensive way to find the ten qualified candidates they assume must be somewhere inside. Should all of them be parsed and extracted to find just those ten?

Facing that challenge (and flying in the face of those facts), some recruiting system vendors simply declared the résumé "dead" and offered alternatives. Many featured "résumé-builders" or "profiling" systems that simply required candidates to type in the database fields themselves, eliminating parsing and extraction.

The HR-XML Consortium was first started to create universally machine-readable field tags for résumés, so that parsing and extraction would require no intelligence beyond understanding the standardized tags. But until the major job boards and corporate employers require their use, XML tags will offer no solution.

Despite those efforts, candidates still just want to cut-and-paste (or attach) their résumés to their applications, and hiring managers still seem to want them. Most of the profiling vendors are now retrofitting résumé processing applications.

Of course, parsing and extracting has long been only one part of the résumé. The other is searching and matching résumés against open reqs. Again, for nearly a decade, the major solution there has been keyword searches against the full text of résumés. Those work fine so long as the recruiter can write a well-formed Boolean search expression. But a complex Boolean search that accurately targets candidates can often require a paragraph or more of terms, including operators like AND, OR, NEAR, and multiple nested expressions. Aside from librarians, few have mastered it.

The New Solutions

Now the electronic recruiting industry is enjoying a phenomenon quite common to the computer industry at large: start-ups scattered across the country, once ignorant of one another, all using various advanced technologies once called "AI" to attack the exact same problem. In short, a genuine industry trend all focused on new ways to deal with résumés. These startups—Burning Glass, EmployOn, Engenium, MohoMine and others—are offering various new solutions.

Engenium may be taking the most innovative approach. Why force all those unstructured documents into a structured database, if you can find the most qualified candidates from the résumés alone without one? While parsing and extracting into a database will always be necessary for tracking candidates, what function do they serve in searching through the ones you've got and matching them to open reqs? And how can we search more effectively than using keywords in Boolean strings?

Engenium may have answers to all those questions. It has a next-generation conceptual matching technology, which means the exact words in the query do not have to appear in a document to get a match. It was created using a blend of Machine Learning, Vector Space Modeling, dynamic indexing and other high-level mathematical models. It works by mapping relationships between each word and every other word in large sets of résumés. This association of words based on the context in which they are used creates a form of numeric "meaning" and "understanding" for the software.

The software takes what it has "learned" and works directly on unstructured résumés, without extracting a database. Getting a "hit" requires only matching the concepts (or hundreds of associated words in context) that each document contains. It uses no pre-written logic (or lists of words or job categories) since these are all dynamically derived from real world documents.

For the recruiter, this means the ability to take the entire text of the job requisition or even the résumé of the last successful incumbent to search the full text of enormous pools of résumés and quickly get matches without parsing or creating a database! Searches do not require perfect queries, Boolean strings, or even a lot of job-specific knowledge. Recruiters can get what they need quickly and be freed to concentrate on more value-added activities, like building relationships with candidates.

Many recruiters have been practicing TRM for years; unfortunately, they are most often outside the corporate recruiting function.

The Link to Talent Relationship Management

Many recruiters have been practicing TRM for years; unfortunately, they are most often outside the corporate recruiting function. Executive headhunters and even contingent recruiters at agencies all spend part of their time networking with successful executives in their particular fields. They learn the executives' career goals and aspirations and their dissatisfactions at their current jobs. They stay in touch, build relationships, and thus rarely start from scratch when a req hits their desk.

Why don't corporate recruiters do this, too? The simple (and clearly honest answer) is they don't have enough time! For twenty years, recruiting automation has been trying to create that time for them. Recognizing that the résumé may never go away and continuing to innovate around methods for processing it will clearly be the key to success. How to know when success has been attained? When corporate recruiters are no longer so bedeviled by résumés and details that they finally have the time to practice Talent Relationship Management.

> "A fine tool is nothing except in a skilled hand."

—Confucious

5

Technology: Changing the Face of Recruitment

TRACEY CLAYBROOKE-FRIEND

Tracey Claybrooke-Friend, a leader in e-cruitment consulting, specializes in increasing user acceptance, strategic sourcing initiatives, and metrics score card design. Highly regarded for her focused work in designing recruitment training programs, building recruitment ROI strategies, and enabling talent relationship marketing programs around ATS systems, she is a recurring columnist for *Employment Management Today,* and founder of Claybrooke and Associates. Ms. Claybrooke-Friend holds a BA, MA, and EdS from the University of Florida and can be reached at Traceymfriend@yahoo.com.

In a recent white paper published by the Talent Market Group, the following comment is made:

> "In the future, recruiting departments will see their CEOs turn to them for advise, guidance, and recommendations on overall corporate financial management and talent investment strategies."

Throughout this white paper, the Talent Market Group makes repeated reference to skills sets such as financial management, budgeting, project management, talent relationship, leveraging technology, management, and marketing. These skills are historically found in strategic staffing organizations, yet they are frequently scattered and overlooked due to the often limited perception of the staffing function.

But as technology enables better management of the operations associated with staffing, the knowledge base required to succeed as a recruiter will move toward that mentioned in the Talent Market Group's white paper. Technology will force staffing professionals to focus on things like metrics-based budgeting, establishing benchmarks appropriate for their organization, calculating return on investment, and projecting talent acquisition timelines against corporate growth strategies.

Technology will force staffing professionals to focus on things like metrics-based budgeting, establishing benchmarks appropriate for their organization, calculating return on investment, and projecting talent acquisition timelines against corporate growth strategies.

To begin the change process, a staffing executive must have a working knowledge of all the human capital management technologies available to them today. These include:

- Applicant tracking systems
- Assessment and profiling
- Alumni networks/referral management systems
- Talent relationship management tools
- Contingent workforce management systems
- Robots and spiders
- Job boards/job posting aggregators
- e-Benefits
- Time and expense tracking systems
- EEO and affirmative action systems
- Workforce/training management systems.

Once the staffing executive understands each of these technological tools, they must address considerations both at the strategic and individual level. These considerations will be the key to success in the future.

Strategic Considerations

1. **What does it take to be successful in their corporate environment?** In other words, how does the organization define whether or not staffing or HR is successful? When is staffing or HR seen as a value-added partner?

2. **What are the organizational resistance factors that would impact rolling out any of these technologies?** Organizational resistance defines the natural roadblocks that may exist as a result of staffing or HR credibility factors, established or non-established business processes, and perceptions of HR that manifest throughout the organization.

3. **How do we successfully implement and apply these tools and services as part of their overall strategy?** Staffing has both operational and strategic performance expectations. Technology now allows us to measure the goals we are trying to accomplish. Together, how one organization may leverage a technology solution may differ greatly from another. The success of these tools depends upon what the organization is trying to accomplish and how these tools fit into the overall equation.

4. **What data can we obtain that may also be valuable for senior management, business development and/or marketing?** Recently, I have been working with an organization that is growing through mergers and acquisitions. As part of this growth, the staffing department is heavily involved in retreading prior employees and hiring new ones. As part of the strategic alignment process, this staffing department is now gathering competitive intelligence for their mergers and acquisitions group. This came as a result of identifying that staffing has been interviewing people from competitive and complimentary business sectors.

5. **How do we measure the success of these programs and use this data to drive organizational change, make future business decisions, and position staffing to become a valued business partner?** Time to hire and source of hire both impact staffing operational excellence. Reporting time to hire as it relates to future business development activities is a strategic measurement. For example, imagine a consulting partner goes and sells a large project. To accomplish this project, it will require hiring twenty more people with a certain skill set. As a staffing partner, I can assist this partner by providing her with the metrics that show how long it took to hire people with this skill set in the past. The staffing manager can use this as a means to shorten the process, or the partner can use this as a tool to construct a plan with realistic resourcing expectations.

6. **How do these tools and metrics drive budgetary considerations?** Metrics can provide us with a quick view as to "what is" and "what is not" working. As a result, we can make better buying decisions.

Individual Considerations

The individual factors that contribute to the changing landscape within staffing are comprised of challenges, changes, skills, and techniques recruiters must learn to be successful in this new environment. These include:

1. **A recruiter's learning aptitude.** Can the recruiter change and learn the required skill sets needed to move from a service to a business partner?

2. **A recruiter's responsibilities within the organization.** Is recruiting this person's full-time job? If it is not, I recommend you explore the value proposition of technology as it relates to each individual's job description.

3. **Understanding and overcoming a recruiter's resistance to utilizing these new tools and resources.** Understanding why a fear or an apathetic response to utilizing new technology exists and creating a program that responds to it are key steps.

4. **The ability to understand and communicate the ROI factors that directly relate to the individual recruiter.** Often when someone presents the value of technology, it is presented with the organization in mind, instead of addressing the "what's in it for me" principle as it relates to the individual. Therefore, the individual may perceive this as another process that will inhibit their productivity.

5. **Examination of the new skills required by the recruitment staff in order to be successful.** This includes: metrics analysis, budgeting, project planning, sales, marketing, etc.

6. **How will these technologies change a recruiter's day-to-day activities?** If a technology goes against the day-to-day workflow process of the recruiter, that user acceptance of the technology solution will be very low. Technology will change processes, but if it changes the process too drastically, the nature of the recruiter is to work around the process.

7. **What type of continuous training and support will be available to enable this change?** User acceptance and embracement is not a one-time shot. It requires continuous training and working toward addressing the "what's in it for me" principle within different groups, new hires, and changing organizations.

As you can begin to see, technology is driving change both at a strategic and individual level. Along with this change is the process of determining whether the current environment you are working in can support or embrace these efforts. The fact of the matter is, these changes will allow staffing professionals to better forecast growth strategies, better manage budgetary constraints, and better communicate successes and resolve issues.

The new staffing professional will be the one to survive during economic up and down times. They are also the individuals who corporate leaders can grow to depend upon.

> "The future ain't what it use to be."

—Yogi Berra

5

How Much You Know About Who: Tips on Digging Deeper

KEVIN WHEELER

Kevin Wheeler, the President and Founder of Global Learning Resources, Inc. (GLR), is a globally-known speaker, author, columnist, and consultant in human capital acquisition and development. His extensive career, global client base, and research affiliations make GLR a leading provider of both strategy and process. Most recently Mr. Wheeler was the Senior Vice President for Staffing and Workplace Development at the Charles Schwab Corporation in San Francisco. He also serves as adjunct faculty at both San Jose State University and San Francisco State University. Mr. Wheeler can be reached at kwheeler@glresources.com.

It's not who you know or what you know that makes you an effective recruiter. Though those things are pluses and will increase the odds that you'll succeed, what really counts is *what* you know about *who*. The more information you have about a candidate, the better you will be able to judge how well they will fit your culture, how reliable and honest they are, or if the skills they claim they have are really there.

The problem we have is getting all that information. Résumés are almost useless. They are advertisements for the candidate and are designed to let a candidate present his strengths and experiences in a positive light. Most recruiters believe that this is what they want, but I think they would rather have other information. For example, wouldn't it be nice to know how deep a candidate's skills really are? Wouldn't it be useful to know if they are reliable, hard working, and so forth?

Most of us, though, spend too much time (and have little success) trying to figure these things out with little success. After all, think of the tools we have to work with. Most of us have boring and ineffective websites that let anyone send in a résumé, use generic job descriptions that allow too much latitude for interpretation, employ tools that allow us to gather résumés but not really get at the information we want, and conduct face-to-face interviews that often fail to extract any additional useful information.

Employee referral programs are popular because we assume that the fellow employee knows the person well enough to vouch for many of these specific, often intangible, qualities that cannot be found on the résumé or in the interview. We assume that the employee has the in-depth knowledge we lack and can't get. But this may be a bad assumption to make, since turnover rates for referrals are probably the same as for those employees you found using other methods. The notion that these programs result in better quality employees at lower cost are most likely just myths. We don't have any well-done studies that would give us empirical data that I know of.

But all hope is not lost. Technology can help, as can other simple techniques for digging deeper instead of wider, as we usually do. I am continually amazed at how many organizations continue to post jobs to job boards when they complain about being swamped with résumés. But if they could mine these résumés, they would find great treasure.

Here are a few tips to get you started down that path:

1. **Make the most of your applicant tracking system.**

   Most large organizations have a résumé tracking system or ATS. While these are mostly useless for the kind of data mining I am suggesting, they can be used more effectively than they are now. Spending time to conduct better searches and broaden or narrow search terms can pay off in identifying more candidates than many recruiters do. In fact, many recruiters are still intimidated by Boolean searches and don't really use their databases well. Get someone to help you if you aren't comfortable doing these searches and take some time to learn how to do them better.

Get your ATS vendor to teach you how to do better searches. Every ATS vendor would be happy to help you in this endeavor—because it will make you a happier customer.

2. **Embrace the power of e-mail.**

When you have identified a potentially good candidate, start an e-mail dialogue with her. Ask questions. Ask for examples and any other data that will inform you enough to make better judgments.

Personal e-mail to candidates is powerful. It flatters the candidate. It makes her feel good to be acknowledged and asked questions. The candidate's response can also make you feel better about your decision whether or not to recommend her to a hiring manager.

If you develop some standard questions—even a template—you can quickly e-mail many candidates with one mouse click. This is far faster and more efficient than the traditional phone call, which often catches the candidate off guard and unprepared.

3. **Build a better website.**

Over the past few weeks I have mentioned many websites that are collecting better data from candidates interactively than they do from the static résumés. Take a look at Chili's interactive interview or at the Boston Consulting Group's interactive case study. Both of these gather rich information about candidates in a way that saves both the recruiter and the candidate a lot of time.

A simple questionnaire can be developed very easily, collect information quickly, and even weight the information according to a weighting scheme you develop, giving you ranked lists of potential candidates.

And all of this helps immensely by removing you from the administrative process of screening hundreds of résumés.

4. **Gather information from many sources.**

   The final tip is simple. Don't just rely on the résumé and interview for information. Check referrals to the extent that you legally can. Develop a format for doing this that asks for specific information and examples, not just vague feelings.

   If the candidate is at a high level, comb newspapers and association literature for any scraps of information that could be useful. For example, reports on promotions or job movement are frequently available in local papers. The candidates may have written articles that could give the hiring manager insight into his interests and strengths. And the candidate may have a personal website that offers additional views and can increase your overall knowledge.

   You can also use your network to ask about the candidates. Has anyone ever heard of him? What have they heard?

   Moving into depth and away from volume is a learning process, but once you are comfortable doing this and have developed the technology and the tools to help you, you will be a much better recruiter for it.

> "I know of no more encouraging fact than the unquestionable ability of man to elevate his life by conscious endeavor."

—Henry David Thoreau

5

Keeping Their Interest: Talent Relationship Management Combines Technology with a Personal Touch to Lure the Best Job Candidates

SHERMAN M. FRIDMAN

Sherman M. Fridman is a retired attorney and highly respected business, technology, lifestyle, and travel writer. Based in Southern California, Mr. Fridman's insightful and timely articles are read worldwide and appear in many publications including *Human Resource Executive*. He is the author of one novel, *The Scorpio Secret*. Mr. Fridman can be reached at fridman@excite.com.

The phrase "War for Talent" is used so often to describe today's hiring process that one can almost hear shells whizzing past the heads of embattled HR executives. But even in a weakened economy, the struggle to capture and retain high-quality talent is an ongoing one. Recently, a new weapon made an appearance on the battlefield. Known as talent relationship management, its purpose is to help companies quickly and efficiently find and hire the most talented people in their respective fields.

These days, it's virtually impossible to open any business publication today without seeing a reference to relationship management. Whether the relationship being managed is with customers or physical assets such as inventories and buildings, or non-tangible items such as intellectual property, software developers have a solution for it.

However, the recruiting space has been slow to optimize the use of technology. In the beginning, the Internet appeared to be a solution for recruiters, who were able to get an enormous amount of résumés via job-board postings and mass e-mail distribution. But HR executives soon learned that sheer quantity is not as important as the ability to cull the best talent from among thousands of applicants. As a result, some companies and software developers are enhancing their electronic recruiting functions to incorporate TRM systems to do for recruiting what customer relationship management does for sales and marketing. Companies with a CRM system can tell which customers are the most profitable, which marketing campaigns deliver the strongest customer response, and which prospects are most likely to buy a particular product.

Today, according to Mark Lange, Vice President of Marketing and Business Development for BrassRing Systems in San Mateo, Calif., TRM systems bring similar benefits to the employment process. And why not? After all, in today's marketplace, obtaining good talent is indeed a sales and marketing activity.

Sustainable Pools

Companies that sell TRM solutions broadly define their product as a suite of applications designed to more effectively manage the hiring process. TRM is not simply the use of digital technology to store and shuffle résumés. Instead, TRM uses technology, as well as personal participation from HR and hiring professionals, to manage a company's relationships with external candidates and existing employees.

The goal is not simply to fill open jobs, but to create a long-term, sustainable talent pool into which the enterprise can reach as positions open up in the future. It's about building personal relationships with a broad range of talent from various sources, including people actively seeking employment as well as passive job seekers. It's also about building relationships with people who have the skills a company is interested in, but for whom no positions currently exist.

Some companies, such as Wayne, PA-based Kenexa Corp., eschew using the term Talent Relationship Management, preferring instead to refer to their package of technology and services as "Human Capital Management." But the goal is essentially the same: To provide efficiencies in the way businesses hire, retain, and manage their human assets.

Ranjan Sinha, CEO of Goodshark Enterprises, a Mountain View, CA-based provider of TRM solutions, says his company's service adds efficiency to the talent-searching process while providing the necessary "human touch." Goodshark's technology builds a talent bank of résumés from various sources, then sends out appropriate responses to each job applicant.

Goodshark's clients can profile where specific applications are coming from and, just as CRM applications can tell an enterprise which marketing campaigns are working, Goodshark's TRM can be used to test the success of various hiring methods by ranking the effectiveness of responses received from various sources, such as outside agencies, job banks, Internet and print ads, or on-line job boards.

However, TRM is not just computer-based applications. It's "a philosophy as much as a technology," says John Sullivan, head of the human resources management program at San Francisco State University.

Sullivan cites two relationship-building functions that are an important part of TRM. The first is TRM's ability to allow companies to "pre-need hire," using the time between identifying a potential employee and a job becoming available to gain further insight into how well that person will fit into the culture of the hiring enterprise as well as the job itself. For example, Sullivan recommends HR invite active and passive job seekers to company events, allowing hiring managers to see how well they interact with current employees. Another option is to ask prospective hires to speak on topics in their areas of expertise at company conferences, or hiring them as consultants for specific projects.

A second function of TRM as described by Sullivan is "personal courting," or the process by which a company lets someone know they're interested in having them come aboard someday. Similar to dating, it involves the parties getting to know each other and building a personal relationship that will, hopefully, give the candidate a favorable impression of the company.

According to Sam Modoono, national director of talent management at the HR practice of Watson Wyatt Worldwide, financial incentives—while important—are not a primary motivator for the can-do superstars most companies are seeking.

Instead, passion and excitement about what a company is trying to accomplish will keep high caliber people talking—and thinking—about coming to work there, even if they're currently employed elsewhere.

"A good organization will pay attention to good relationships," Modoono says. "It's a highly connected kind of thing."

Getting to Know You

According to BrassRing's Lange, there are three basic functions of any TRM program: Identify active and passive job seekers, cultivate a relationship between company and talent, and then market the company to the candidate.

Enabling the identification of job seekers—active or passive—is where digital technology reigns supreme. While some perform certain functions better than others do, all top-of-the-line integrated TRM application suites have similar capabilities. They can comb the Internet for résumés, identify key employees of a company, and access staff directories or contact lists of other companies to seek out passive job seekers. TRM applications can also assist the search process by finding key words, links to websites, and references.

These applications—which are generally web-based and give 24/7 access to information from anywhere using a browser—also contain a candidate database that stores all of an HR department's information on job candidates. In addition to on-line searches, this database is supplied with information from many other channels, including job boards, recruiting agencies, résumés submitted directly to the company, and employee referral programs. Passive job seekers are identified by sophisticated search engines that allow people with specific characteristics to be targeted, whether they're located on Internet job sites, trade association websites, or personal and company-specific web pages.

But the full benefit of a TRM suite is not realized by just collecting résumés; it comes in the establishment of a relationship, particularly with people for whom there are no presently available openings. This process can be as simple as sending a job applicant an automatic e-mail confirming receipt of a résumé, or it can extend to such levels of sophistication as tracking and acknowledging the career and personal milestones of an industry superstar whom a company is trying to woo.

One example cited by Sullivan is keeping track of the school graduation dates of courted candidates' children, since that's generally the time when parents are most receptive to relocating. Or, during a particularly bad snowstorm, a company based in Southern California might contact a sought-after executive living in Chicago whose hobby is boating, reminding the person of the lifestyle advantages in moving to the West Coast.

Sullivan describes these bits of knowledge as forming part of a company's "competitive intelligence." It's not difficult to do when the parameters of an e-recruitment database have been structured so potential employees can be selected by many different criteria, such as zip code, hobbies, and alma mater, in addition to job skills. But competitive intelligence is based upon personal knowledge that can't be gotten solely from a computer.

For example, an industry superstar may have has just gotten a divorce, making it the perfect time to entice him or her to start over in a new city, with a new company. But this information doesn't come from TRM software; it comes from the HR professional's or hiring manager's personal knowledge of their industry and the important people in it.

"If your company doesn't know who the top talent in its industry is, you're in trouble," says Sullivan. He suggests that such talent be tracked continuously so that when an opportunity presents itself, it can be seized upon. Even acknowledging a competing executive's promotion can create a favorable impression that may translate into giving your company the edge in hiring this superstar in the future.

Most companies don't go to such extremes; but many do make an effort to maintain relationships with their talent base. Dan Guaglianone, Vice President of Recruiting and Staffing worldwide for Unisys, the Blue Bell, PA-based provider of e-business solutions, says his company, like others, is just now learning the most effective way to establish relationships. Guaglianone says Unisys' approach is very simple: A list is kept of candidates the company is interested in hiring and periodically a recruiter will telephone people on the list to stay in touch and update their contact information. Unisys also sends out e-mail with company news to potential employees.

Nicole Stata, Founder and CEO of Deploy Solutions Inc. in Westwood, MA, says that her company's suite of HR applications has a built-in "Candidate Hot List" that allows HR professionals to keep in touch with candidates for whom no jobs are presently available. When a job opens up that matches a candidate's particular skills, that candidate is automatically contacted.

Robyn Mingle, Vice President of Human Resources for Towson, MD-based Decker, uses an informal "touch-base mentality" in reaching out to people she would like to hire, telling them to "let me know where you are." Mingle also stays in touch by sending e-mail every four to six months to specially selected individuals who've indicated they wouldn't mind the contact.

Regardless of the various levels of sophistication that can be employed to establish and maintain relationships with prospective employees, e-mail is the most basic way companies stay in touch. It's fast, virtually free, and easily scalable. But one caution: e-mail has to be used judiciously, and only with people who have "opted-in" to receive such communications. Otherwise, warns Sean Magennis, President of North American operations for Dallas-based human resources consultant Thomas International, "it becomes just a marketing gimmick."

"[The technology] is only as good as the people who are using it," says Zach Thomas, Kenexa's product manager. In other words, the hiring professional must have the skills to analyze the talent data and decide upon the appropriate course of action to take.

Obviously, the time, effort, and money expended on establishing and managing a TRM program depends on how essential the company views the talent being recruited. But, advises Unisys' Guaglianone, "TRM is a very important piece of what any company is going to have to be good at in the future."

CHAPTER SIX

Aligning Talent Metrics for C-Level Decision-Making

> "You miss 100 percent of the shots you never take."

—Wayne Gretsky

6

Metrics and the Metrics Driven Staffing Model

STEVE LAMOTTA

Steve LaMotta is Vice President of HRAlliance. Prior to this he was President of Staffing.org and was a senior business development and strategic solutions executive for the Bernard Hodes Group and People Solutions, Inc. Mr. LaMotta is an advisor to several state and national human resource organizations and is currently an EMA Foundation board member. He co-chairs the HR Boardroom, a senior human resource executive group forum and is a frequent speaker on human resource practices. Best known for his strategic solutions and human resource architecture, Mr. LaMotta can be reached at slamotta@thehra.com.

We are in the midst of the most competitive employment market in over twenty years—recruiters never had it so good. Compensation for corporate recruiters has jumped from the bottom of the HR hierarchy to the top. Recruiting contractors and consultants are billing at extraordinary rates. But wait, what a difference a year makes! That was then and this is now. . . in a matter of months and now approaching a year—"the proverbial worm has turned"—the marketplace worm that is. The collapse of the technology sector, dot-bombs making the news and venture capital firms demanding that they start making money. No more nice guys and cool Internet driven business concepts. They want a return-on-investment. Imagine that!

So for now, recruiting contractors and consultants are left without job orders and jobs. They are being pushed out, for some, forced out of business and staffing departments are slashing costs—people costs. And yet the recruiters that are left "in the game" still complain that they are not respected and management laments how long and how much it costs to fill jobs—at least the few jobs that are open. Why?

Recruiting is still practiced and measured as more of an art than a science. Recruiting has lacked valid metrics and an operating model. What you do not measure does not count and any endeavor requires a model from which to build. Doesn't matter whether it's a boom period or a bust backlash—Staffing has lacked both.

Part I: The Metrics—Its Time has Come!

There are four key issues in evaluating recruiters and the staffing function according to Staffing.org, (www.staffing.org) the leading non-profit staffing metrics' organization.

These are cost efficiency, time efficiency, customer satisfaction, and quality. The current available measures include cost-per-hire, time to fill and time to start, customer satisfaction surveys, and basic retention numbers. Unfortunately all the current measures have deficiencies. For example, the cost-per-hire does not take into account significant geographic and industry differences. Nor does everyone calculate it consistently.

Retention numbers, which are sometimes used to measure quality, cannot effectively separate quality hires from quality employees. And more often than not, there is no measurement of the recruiting function.

The metrics driven staffing model is a four-part metric that is broader in scope and overcomes the deficiencies of the current measures. This four-part metric measures each of the key issues using the following criteria:

Key Issue	Four-Part Metric Measure
Cost efficiency	Recruiting efficiency ratio
Time efficiency	Staffing time ratio
The customer	Customer satisfaction survey results
Quality	Performance check and new hire quality surveys six to eighteen months

Quality Measure

Quality in the metrics driven staffing model is measured by tracking the performance evaluation rating of new hires between six and eighteen months, tracking the retention of highly rated new hires at twelve to eighteen months, and determining the sources of highly rated and retained hires.

Customer Satisfaction Measure

Customer satisfaction is measured by surveying the customers in the recruiting process. While this process will include surveying the hiring managers, it may include other customer groups such as new hires and those candidates who have declined an offer. Once a survey is taken, it is important to be prepared to respond to insights from the survey, make changes, and provide status and metric reports to customers on a regular basis.

Time Efficiency Measure

The four-part metric uses the staffing time ratio to determine the time efficiency measure. This ratio is calculated as:

Staffing Time Ratio = Actual/Contracted Time to Fill

Measuring time using this ratio does not assume that all positions should take the same time to fill. It encourages and requires that recruiters have a planning session before the search begins and allows them to set realistic expectations with hiring managers . . . otherwise known as becoming a "true business partner."

Cost Efficiency

Cost efficiency is measured using the Recruiting Efficiency Ratio and calculated as:

Recruiting Efficiency Ratio = Total Recruiting Costs/Adjusted Compensation Recruited

The terms in this ratio are defined as:

1. **Total Recruiting Costs:**

   Calculated monthly fixed internal costs or "overhead" expense (e.g., recruiter salaries, benefits, technology expense, workspace allocation, etc.)

   \+ **External costs spent to fill a specific position** (e.g., ads, Internet resources/job boards, third party fees, sourcing, etc.)

   \+ **Sign-on Bonuses** (even if it's charged back to the operating unit)

   \+ **Travel, Relocation, and VISA expenses**

   = **Total Recruiting Costs**

2. **Adjusted Compensation Recruited:**

   Compensation of positions filled internally / 4*

   \+ **Compensation of positions filled externally** (base salaries)

   = **Total Adjusted Compensation Recruited**

   * Internally filled positions typically cost one-quarter of an externally filled position.

The Recruiting Efficiency Ratio reflects the correlation between compensation, geographical differences, and candidate supply and demand. It also takes into account that in most cases the higher the pay the more costly it is to fill the position. In other words, it "speaks the language of business" by operationalizing it to reflect market fluctuations by indexing the data. This index is an efficiency measure . . . defined as the amount of costs relative to the amount of human capital assets acquired. (e.g., according to the *Staffing 2000 & 2001: Staffing Performance Report the average company spent approximately 16 cents and 13½ cents respectively of every dollar of compensation or human capital acquired/recruited*.) The table on the next page gives an example of how the Recruiting Efficiency Ratio is superior to the traditional Cost-Per-Hire measure.

Part II: The Staffing Model

In order to get good results with the four-part metrics the staffing function should be patterned after a proven model. The following model includes a recruiting process, the customer alignment of

Positions filled	Total recruiting cost	Total compensation cost	No. of positions filled	Traditional cost-per-hire comparison	Recruiting efficiency ratio %
Customer service reps	$1,000,000	$10,000,000	500	$2,000	10% or spent 10 cents of every dollar of compensation recruited
Software engineer	$600,000	$600,000	100	$6,000	10%

recruiters, the infrastructure, recruiting expertise, staffing consultant skills, and the highest level of partnership between the staffing function and the business.

Closed Loop Recruiting Process

This process is the foundation of the metrics driven staffing model. It looks at staffing as a process rather than a task and also serves as a process for planning and development. The closed loop process has six features, which include:

- **Retain:** becoming the employer of choice for those employees that you want to keep.
- **Attract:** identifying and creating key attraction opportunities and developing models that promote the organization as an employer of choice and its "brand."
- **Select:** selecting the best candidates for each open position.
- **Facilitate Entry:** facilitating entry of new hires into the organization in order to expedite rapid peak performance, career satisfaction, and retention.
- **Evaluate and Change:** evaluating the staffing process to recommend and implement change to the staffing process to effect improvement in creating an efficient return-on-investment.

Customer Aligned Recruiters

The staffing specialists invariably perform better when aligned by customer.

Infrastructure

A staffing infrastructure is necessary due to the process-intensive nature of staffing. Establishing a staffing infrastructure frees up staffing specialists and hiring managers to do what they need to do. It can also reduce the cycle time and improve efficiency. The infrastructure of a staffing function can be divided into operations, sourcing and research, and administration.

Recruiting Expertise

Recruiting expertise has four components: the staffing related competencies that expert recruiters have; training programs to help recruiters become experts; performance standards that serve as guidelines for staffing specialists' behavior; and a monthly performance summary to determine the level of expertise. Having expert recruiters in the staffing department creates credibility with hiring managers, develops greater flexibility in staffing and results in increased job satisfaction for staffing specialists.

Staffing Consultant Skills

This refers to the skills that the staffing specialist need to get information about an opening from the hiring managers, address and solve problems in the hiring process, and influence those involved in the hiring process.

Ultimate Customer Partnership

The goal is to reach the ultimate customer partnership; you know you are there when *your customer views you* as someone who achieves business objectives, transfers knowledge, builds understanding, bonds people and organizations, and drives meaningful change.

It's all about performance and the resulting ROI to the business!

> "When everyone is thinking alike, then no one is thinking."

—General George S. Patton

6

The Difference Between Rightsizing and Wrongsizing

BARBARA DAVISON

Barbara Davison is a Principal Consultant with Saratoga Institute, subsidiary of Spherion Corporation. Her background encompasses over twenty-five years in human resources management. Since 1982, she has managed her own consulting firm in addition to her full-time consulting positions with Saratoga Institute. As one of the founding members of the company, she helped to formulate the research, development, publication, and training of staff measurement, benchmarking, and performance evaluation practices that demonstrate financial value. Ms. Davison has authored five publications offered through the American Management Association/AMACOM and her most recent book is the third edition of *How to Measure Human Resources Management*, co-authored with Dr. Jac Fitz-enz. Ms. Davison can be reached at BarbaraDavison@saratoga-institute.com.

Cutting staff is a common response during economic downturns, but if staffing plans aren't linked to business strategy, rightsizing can go badly wrong.

Decreased sales, increased competition, economic downturn, lost customers, cost-cutting mandates, and disproportionate workforces. These are some of the sad facts of business life today. In the response to these challenges, many businesses are repositioning and reallocating both human and financial resources through a process called "rightsizing."

Rightsizing, or "resizing" as it's currently known, takes on many different meanings within organizations. It can mean reducing the workforce, "downsizing" or eliminating functions, reducing expenses, or redesigning systems and policies. It can also involve "upsizing" (increasing the workforce in certain areas), and "sidesizing" (repositioning the workforce to other areas). Unfortunately, it can also include "wrongsizing," or losing key talent that a company can't afford to lose.

These days, workforce reduction is one of the most common rightsizing activities—a decision sometimes driven by the need for short-term profits. According to consulting firm Challenger, Gray and Christmas, close to two million jobs in the US were lost in 2001. The firm reported an additional 255,000 job cuts in first quarter of 2002. And it's not over.

Unfortunately, if rightsizing is simply being done to reduce costs, it will have minimal, and perhaps only momentary, impact on the organization. Eliminating people without first having a method for determining how many were needed to begin with is a short-term solution that is bound to create the same crisis over again and in a very short time. According to management consultant Anthony Tasca, co-founder of SKOPOS, the difference between rightsizing and downsizing is that the former is a strategic planning step and the latter is simply a reaction to earlier mistakes.

Rightsizing works when it is part of a planned reinvention of a company that pays attention to its business strategy, cost implications, and human capital issues. In contrast to across-the-board layoffs, a good rightsizing program looks for improvements in

The difference between rightsizing and downsizing is that the former is a strategic planning step and the latter is simply a reaction to earlier mistakes.

organizational productivity and effectiveness through redesign of business processes.

A successful "rightsizing" effort, therefore, is significantly more than cost or headcount reductions. It often reduces work as well as costs. It often involves doing more work with fewer resources. It seeks to reduce costs and improve organizational productivity by redesigning processes and organization structures. The intended result is that resources are focused on core competencies that produce competitive advantage.

To be successful in the long term, rightsizing must be tied to overall strategy and identify critical growth areas as well as those needing consolidation. Rightsizing is a dynamic process and must be continually evaluated. It cannot establish an exact headcount number. Instead, it is dependent upon continual improvements to processes and structures in order to meet strategic objectives and improve productivity.

Key Considerations

Deciding why and how to rightsize an organization are as important as deciding what to rightsize.

The first step is clarifying the organization's vision and position. Then it is necessary to look at the market that the organization is trying to serve. As every organization is a unique combination of stakeholders, competitors, and market position factors, a decision to rightsize staff or processes directly relates to the organization's unique model. Only after assessing that unique model should business leaders consider the size and composition of the staff. At this point, decisions either to keep or lay off, retrain or reassign, can be made with a purpose and set of goals in mind.

Rightsizing, therefore, requires establishing clear priorities and asking objective questions. The answers become the foundation and premise upon which the rightsizing plan is based and provide the hard data and knowledge not only to make appropriate decisions but also to measure the results.

Questions to consider include the following:

1. How will the changes affect Marketing (programs, product awareness, and partnerships)?

2. What effects will be seen on Sales and Customer Service (sales efficiency, quotas, customer coverage, and customer acquisition)?
3. What are the consequences to Product Development (development schedules, cost, product quality)?
4. What are the Finance implications (reporting systems and vendors)?
5. How will Manufacturing and Operations be affected (product costs, delivery schedules, and product quality)?
6. What are the effects on Human Capital (revenue per employee; morale, retention, incentives for remaining employees; external message, severance costs, health benefit requirements and costs)?
7. What is the return on capital expended to make the reductions (resizing value, revenue impact, margins and/or profits, tax implications, and return on assets)?
8. What are our alternatives (retraining, redeployment, reduced work hours, outsourcing)?

Measuring Human Capital

A key element in the strategy to rightsize or change the face of the organization is the mandate that each department and employee must add measurable value. This is where HR plays a pivotal role. The HR team can give the CEO and CFO a powerful understanding of the role human capital plays in the organization and the way it combines with business processes to expand or shrink shareholder value. This business partnership and information about the organization's human capital is vital to making the "right" rightsizing decisions.

Since employee costs can often exceed 40 percent of organizational expense, measuring and managing human capital is critical to maximizing business results. A good starting point is to understand the following factors:

- Market pressures affecting the organization
- Financial status
- Strategic initiatives
- Corporate culture
- Management's philosophy

Each of these factors directly or indirectly relates to an employee's ability to perform.

A company's human capital is in a state of constant change. Employees come and go, knowledge is acquired, skills developed, and relationships rise and fall. In order to see and measure this fluctuation, management uses a system of quantitative and qualitative metrics that describe and predict the cost and productivity curves of its workforce.

Quantitative measures generally focus on cost, quantity, and time. Qualitative measures center on perceived value/quality and human reaction/satisfaction. The quantitative measures explain what happened, and the qualitative provide some idea of why. Combined, they present insights into the causes and results of certain activities and behaviors.

As an example, say a company's costs or delivery times are increasing, most likely as a result of quality problems. Product defects are not only causing rework and slowing delivery time, but they are also spurring customers to look for other suppliers. Fewer customers means revenue is down and marketing costs are up, which in turn means product cost and overall operating expenses are escalating. An effective measurement system for this company would include metrics that track the linkages between delivery times, costs, and revenues, that can be trended over time, and that allow for business unit, divisional, and department breakdowns.

The way to develop sound measurement systems is to (1) focus on quality, efficiency, and service; and, (2) use the five factors that can be applied to anything you choose to measure: cost, time, quantity, quality, and human reaction/satisfaction. The business case is to think about the logic of where the organization is now and where it wants to go rather than the measurement. When going through a rightsizing, a company would use metrics to:

1. Determine what needs to change
2. Focus the direction of the change
3. Monitor the effects.

If the move is aimed at improving customer service, that should be measured. If it is targeted toward cost reduction, use metrics that drive the change in that direction.

Rightsizing Metrics: The Human and Financial Connection

Quite a number of rightsizing programs start at the business unit level. This is a mistake. Value can be seen and created only if the entire organization's business objectives and strategic goals are the starting point. The business units or departments must establish and link their service, quality, and productivity objectives to the organization's financial, market, and human goals. The actions of people determine whether or not business unit goals are achieved, which then determines if organizational goals are successful. Metrics on the tactical level measure improvements or change in human capital performance, and monitor human capital effects on business unit objectives. Strategic level metrics show the effects of human capital on organizational goals. Some examples of strategic human capital metrics are listed at the end of this article.

There are many tools available to forge the link between human and financial performance, as part of evaluating, setting, and managing a rightsizing program—as well as measuring its success or failure. One is the balanced scorecard. This is a proven process that helps organizations translate their goals and objectives into targeted actions. Usually encompassing four sets of performance measures, the scorecard displays how employees, financial performance, customers/markets, and operating efficiencies all affect one another and have an impact on shareholder value.

These performance measures can be leading or lagging indicators and predictors of future success as well as quantifiable measures of past performance. The balanced scorecard can be customized to the organizations strategic objectives. What to measure and how to measure varies, depending on each organization's business and operations.

Aligning Human Capital to the Business

There are six basic steps that can help you in the process of aligning current or projected human capital to the organization's new strategic business goals and objectives:

Step 1. **Establish business objectives and strategic goals.** Because business is dynamic, aligning the employee's competencies and performance goals requires constant reassessment of strategy and direction.

Step 2. **Communicate the business objectives and goals.** Leaders need to communicate the message clearly and frequently. And they need to translate objectives into specific tasks that employees can understand and accept.

Step 3. **Align the organization structure to the new business objectives and goals.** The organization's structure has to allow for goal achievement. This includes department staffing levels, number and types of staff, and competencies required.

Step 4. **Assess Human Capital Readiness.** Evaluate the employee's readiness to meet the competencies required. This includes skills, knowledge, ability, and behaviors.

Step 5. **Gap Analysis.** The results of the four steps listed above will point out where you have gaps that need to be addressed to assure successful alignment with the business. What additional skills, knowledge, ability, and behaviors are needed to achieve alignment?

Step 6. **Implement, Measure, Evaluate, Analyze, Link, Predict, Act.** This last step is at the heart of any successful strategy execution and rightsizing effort. Plans need to be continually evaluated for applicability and effectiveness.

A Rightsizing Process Example

If rightsizing becomes necessary, there is a basic process that can be followed to determine the extent of the reductions and minimize the damage. Keep in mind that the metrics need to be included in each step of the process. Without the quantitative data, one cannot measure the success of the program.

The elements of the rightsizing process are:

- Based on clear business objectives and strategies, develop scenarios of what the business will look like, both in the short term and the long term. What are the implications for the skills and numbers of employees as well the necessary organizational structure?
- Assess the skill sets of current employees and the impact of average separation rates on staff levels. Include current and predicted labor market conditions to assess hiring difficulties, including availability, time to fill, and costs.

- If workforce excess is indicated, try to place current skilled employees in any open positions or transfer them into areas expected to need additional staff within the next six to twelve months. If the employees cannot be retained, outplacement services are an excellent way to "soften the blow" and still maintain employer reputation.
- Communicate to all levels as frequently as possible the business conditions and organization strategy and process that resulted in the decision to reduce staff.
- Develop a severance package that is as comprehensive and generous as is possible. Treating departing employees well and with respect has a positive impact on the employees who remain and the company's reputation as a whole.
- Communicate the severance, outplacement, and rehire programs and incentives to all employees before discussing it with the affected employees. This gives employees and management time to assess individual situations and make modifications if necessary.
- After the layoffs have been completed, have follow-up meetings with employees to communicate the results and reaffirm the organization's strategy.
- Maintain contact with the displaced employees either through direct communication, e-mail, newsletters, or an employee information portal.

If a rightsizing or downsizing becomes an annual process, you undoubtedly did not do a complete analysis the first time. Employer reputation and management integrity will suffer.

The rightsizing that Ernst and Young recently experienced was made more palatable to employees through some creative options. E&Y, number eighty-seven on Fortune's list of "Best Companies to Work For," redeployed people to other areas, loaned staff to clients experiencing temporary shortages, and offered voluntary leaves of absence at 25 percent of pay. Schwab, number forty-six on the list, laid off 3,800 employees and offered up to eight months of severance, a corporate alumni network, and one of the most successful outplacement programs reported.

Cisco, another innovative company, paid employees one-third of their salary if they chose to work for a social service agency, paid full benefits, and put affected employees on a priority hiring list that would be used when the company started hiring again.

Agilent Technologies has been recognized as one of the most successful companies dealing with severe cutbacks. Good management, good planning, and empathy all played a role. CEO Ned Barnholt kept in constant communication with all employees regarding strategy and results as well as empowering employees to take their own initiatives on cost cutting.

Alternatives to Resizing

There are many alternatives to resizing and downsizing the workforce. As organizations face this unending battle, new choices are being offered that allow them to be creative and look for other alternatives. Some areas to take into account include:

- Cross training
- Succession planning
- Outsourcing
- Job sharing
- Retraining (making vs. buying)
- Redeployment within the organization
- Creating revenue enhancement opportunities (employee created)

- Reduced hours
- Lower compensation
- Planned attrition
- Early retirement
- Retention bonus
- Leave of absence
- Employee buyouts (employees purchase functions slated to close)
- Shared ownership (employees trade pay increases or pay cuts for company stock)

A New Workforce Concept

Taking a cue from "just-in-time" inventory systems, new research is being conducted to establish the "just-in-time" workforce. This may be a solution to the up-and-down flux of layoffs and rehires.

The concept centers on a "portfolio" of human capital where individuals can be accessed easily and put into place quickly to meet planned and unplanned business requirements. The Portfolio Workforce includes full- and part-time core employees as well as a collective group of contingent staff. The Portfolio Workforce is developed and aligned with the organization's short- and long-term goals and strategies. Development aspects include workforce planning, career development, succession planning, leadership development, and training. Alignment aspects include employee skills, knowledge, and behaviors, as well as quality of work/life initiatives.

The work/life choices are a key component in the program. These choices include accelerated, phased-in work hours for certain groups of employees, and decreased, phased-out work hours for other groups—both of which can change over time as the employee and organization needs evolve. Technically, procedurally, and managerially, the Portfolio Workforce system requires:

- Data, information, and communication
- Assessment of requirements
- Outsourcing options
- Predictive modeling
- Flexible structures and boundaries
- Improved methods of controlling costs and creating value.

The benefits of a Portfolio Workforce are similar to those that are well known by users of the just-in-time systems—reduced cycle times, reduced layoffs, freed-up capital, improved productivity, and increased competitive position. The ideal scenario is the creation of a flexible organization that can respond to business challenges by moving appropriate resources where they will have greatest value. This requires a management team committed to working across functional boundaries.

It's Never Over

An ongoing and continual effort is what keeps an organization's resources focused. As Jack Welch, former CEO of General Electric, stated in his book, *Jack: Straight from the Gut*, "These downsizings are awful, as hardworking people get hammered by competitive change. In difficult businesses these changes never end. I can't tell you how often I was asked in the early 1980s, 'Is it over now?' Unfortunately, it's never over."

Nevertheless, if rightsizing is done intelligently, it can significantly improve organizational efficiency and effectiveness.

Strategic Human Capital Metrics

- Revenue Factor = Total revenue divided by FTEs (full-time equivalent employees). Dollars of revenue generated per FTE is the broadest measure of productivity.
- Sales Factor = Total sales divided by FTEs. Another view of productivity.
- Human Economic Value Added = Net operating profit after tax less cost of capital divided by FTEs. Shows the dollar amount of profit per employee that is left after paying all expenses, including taxes, and subtracting the cost of invested capital.
- Return on Capital Employed = Net profit divided by shareholders equity. Shows the value of human capital from a financial viewpoint.
- Human Capital Cost Factor = Compensation plus benefit costs, contingent staff costs, absenteeism cost, and cost of turnover divided by FTEs. Shows the base costs of an organization's human capital and provides a more descriptive view of labor than simply compensation and benefit costs per employee.
- Human Capital Value Added = Revenue minus operating expense (less compensation and benefit costs) divided by FTEs. A better view of productivity, which shows the average profitability per employee.
- Human Capital ROI = Revenue minus operating expense (less compensation and benefit costs) divided by compensation and benefit costs. Shows the ROI in terms of profit for dollars spent on employee compensation and benefits.
- Human Capital Productivity Factor = Total assets divided by FTEs. Provides a dollar asset value per employee.
- Management Ratio = Employee headcount divided by management headcount. Shows the average number of employees to each manager. Also known as span of control.
- Exempt Percent = Exempt FTEs divided by total FTEs. Shows what percent of the workforce is an exempt level employee. Can also be broken down by job group.

In addition, consider the Saratoga Institute Standard Key Performance Indicators (KPIs). These are twelve macro-level metrics that all HR organizations should be measuring and reporting. They provide a top-level view of the organization's health and can easily be added to a scorecard.

1. Revenue per Employee
2. Expense per Employee
3. Income per Employee
4. Human Capital ROI
5. Management Ratio
6. HR Headcount Ratio
7. Training Cost Factor
8. Benefit Factor
9. Healthcare Factor
10. Employee Cost Factor
11. Cost per Hire
12. Voluntary Separation Rate

Appendix

Grateful acknowledgement to publishers and authors below for permission to reprint the following in this anthology:

"Executing Organizational Strategy Through a Talent-Focused Culture" by Jennifer A. Chatman PhD. Copyright © 2002 by Jennifer A. Chatman PhD. All rights reserved. Portions of this paper were excerpted from Chatman, J. & Cha, S. (forthcoming, 2003). Leading through leveraging culture. To appear in, S. Chowdhury (Ed.), Next Generation Business Series: Leadership, Financial Times-Prentice Hall Publishers. Reprinted with permission from author.

"Automating Employment Management: TRM, the New Generation" by H. Michael Boyd PhD. Copyright © 2002 by H. Michael Boyd PhD. All rights reserved. Reprinted with permission from author.

"Talent Relationship Management—The Last Source of Competitive Advantage" by Mark Lange. First appeared in IHRIM Journal, May 2002. Copyright © 2002 by IHRIM Journal. All rights reserved. Reprinted with permission from the publisher and author.

"The Corporate ROI of Direct Contractor Engagement" by Matthew Bender and Austin Whitman. Copyright © 2002 by Contractors Resources, Inc. and BrassRing LLC. All rights reserved. Reprinted with permission from publishers and author.

"In the Trenches: Talent Relationship Management for the Everyday Recruiter" by Patrick Lewsen. Copyright © 2002 by Patrick Lewsen. All rights reserved. Reprinted with permission from author.

"The 3 Dimensions of Diversity Recruiting On-line" by Peter Weddle. Copyright © 2002 by *WEDDLE's*, Peter Weddle. All rights reserved. Reprinted with permission from author.

"The Human Element of Recruiting" by Ken Gaffey first appeared on the Electronic Recruiting Exchange http://www.erexchange.com, May 21, 2002. Copyright © 2002 by Electronic Recruiting Exchange and Ken Gaffey. All rights reserved. Reprinted with permission from publisher and author.

"The Value of Relationships in Your Talent Inventory" by Cary Smith first appeared on the Electronic Recruiting Exchange http://www.erexchange.com, November 6, 2001. Copyright © 2001 by Electronic Recruiting Exchange and Cary Smith. All rights reserved. Reprinted with permission from publisher and author.

"Winning the Talent War with a TRM Hiring Strategy" by Lou Adler. Copyright © 2002 by POWER Hiring, Lou Adler. All rights reserved. Reprinted with permission from author.

"Antidote to High Turnover: Talent Relationship Management" by Gregory P. Smith. Copyright © 2002 by Chart Your Course International, Gregory P. Smith. All rights reserved. Reprinted with permission of author.

"Executive Coaching: Retention Tool in Uncertain Times" by Jeffrey M. Cohen. Copyright © 2002 by Jeffrey M. Cohen. All rights reserved. Reprinted with permission from author.

"Rehabilitating the Problem Employee" by Lawrence M. Bienati PhD. Copyright © 2002 by Lawrence M. Bienati PhD. All rights reserved. Reprinted with permission from author.

"TRM's Number 2 Dilemma" by Ed Newman. Copyright © 2002 by Ed Newman. All rights reserved. A variation of this article appeared in *News for Recruiters*, Issue 060202, Vol. 2002. Reprinted with permission from publisher and author.

"Leadership Strategies for TRM" by Jac Fitz-enz PhD. Copyright © 2002 by Jac Fitz-enz PhD. All rights reserved. Reprinted with permission from author.

"As Generation X-ers Enter the Workplace, HR Remains in the Hospital" by Alfred J. Walker. First appeared in *IHRIM.link*, February/March 2001. Copyright © 2001 by *IHRIM.link*. All rights reserved. Reprinted with permission from publisher and author.

"Getting Up from Down" by Robert J. McGarvey first appeared in *American Way* Magazine, the inflight publication of American Airlines, June 2002. Copyright © 2002 Robert J. McGarvey. All rights reserved. Reprinted with permission from publisher and author.

"Employee Loyalty: It's Your Business" by Keith A. Lavine. Copyright © 2002 by Keith A. Lavine. All rights reserved. Reprinted with permission from author.

"Creating Organizational Justice: Where Talent Relationship Management Meets Employment Liability" by Joni E. Johnston PsyD. Copyright © 2002 by Joni E. Johnston, PsyD. All rights reserved. Reprinted with permission from author.

"Managing the Resource Pool: The Right and the Wrong Way to Manage Human Capital" by Gary A. Bolles. Copyright © 2002 by Gary A. Bolles. All rights reserved. Reprinted with permission from author.

"Why Top Talent Looks Elsewhere" by John Boudreau PhD; Wendy Boswell PhD; Benjamin Dunford, Paul R. Ray, Jr. Copyright © 2001 by John Boudreau PhD, Wendy R. Boswell PhD; Benjamin Dunford, Paul R. Ray, Jr. All rights reserved. Reprinted with permission from authors.

"The Devil Is in the Details" by William M. Kutik. Copyright © 2002 William A. Kutik. All rights reserved. Reprinted with permission from author.

"Technology: Changing the Face of Recruitment" by Tracey Claybrooke-Friend first appeared on the Electronic Recruiting Exchange http://www.erexchange.com, April 12, 2002. Copyright © 2002 by Electronic Recruiting Exchange and Tracey Claybrooke-Friend. All rights reserved. Reprined with permission from publisher and author.

"How Much You Know About Who: Tips on Digging Deeper" by Kevin Wheeler first appeared in the Electronic Recruiting Exchange http://www.erexchange.com, May 29, 2002. Copyright © 2002 by

Electronic Recruiting Exchange and Kevin Wheeler. All rights reserved. Reprinted with permission from publisher and author.

"Keeping Their Interest" by Sherman M. Fridman first appeared in *Human Resource Executive* Magazine, August 2001. Copyright © 2001 by *Human Resource Executive* Magazine. All rights reserved. Reprinted with permission from publisher and author.

"Metrics & the Metrics Driven Staffing Model" by Steve LaMotta first appeared in *CareerXroads 2002*. Copyright © 2002 by Steve LaMotta and the co-authors of *CareerXroads*, Gerry Crispin and Mark Mehler. Reprinted with permission from publisher and author.

"The Difference Between Rightsizing and Wrongsizing" by Barbara Davison first appeared in the *Journal of Business Strategy*, July/August 2002. Copyright © 2002 by *Journal of Business Strategy*. All rights reserved. Reprinted with permission from publisher and author.